In Waiting

In Waiting

Travels in the Shadow of Edwin Muir

Michael W Russell

Neil Wilson Publishing • Glasgow • Scotland

First published by
Neil Wilson Publishing
303a The Pentagon Centre
36 Washington Street
GLASGOW
G3 8AZ
Tel: 0141-221-1117
Fax: 0141-221-5363
E-mail: nwp@cqm.co.uk
http://www.nwp.co.uk/

© Michael W Russell, 1998

The author has established his moral right
to be identified as the author of this work.

A catalogue record for this book is
available from the British Library.

All extracts from Scottish Journey © Gavin Muir
and Mainstream Publishing are reproduced by
kind permission of Mainstream Publishing in
lieu of Gavin Muir's unknown whereabouts.

ISBN 1-897784-63-5

Typeset in Stone Serif and Helvetica Condensed
Designed by Mark Blackadder
Printed by WSOY, Finland

For my father, who wanted more but for whom the time wasn't right
and for Cailean in the hope that it soon will be.

Contents

Acknowledgements

This book is not a political statement, an outline of a political philosophy or an exposition of political policy. No doubt it will be combed and attacked by those who want to make out that it is – but what I have tried to do is simply to travel, talk, listen and think. It is, in Muir's own words, 'a Scottish journey' – one of many. It is also my Scottish journey. Although I hope it is entertaining and thought-provoking, I have no deep ambitions or intentions other than to record and comment. Spin doctors take note.

I am grateful to all those who spoke to me during my travels – many asked not be named and many others were neither asked for their identity, nor did they offer it; so it is with many journeys – and perhaps they are the better for it.

There might be (there should be) an old Chinese proverb that says 'A man who travels on his own learns much about his companion'. But he also learns much about the country through which he travels, and that learning has been made much more enjoyable by those who many years ago awoke an enthusiasm in me for this country and its history, particularly my late father Tom Russell, his brother John Russell and my first history teacher, the enthusiastic Major Cooper (although what he was a major of, I never found out!).

Translating that enthusiasm into a concern not just for the past, but for the future as well, has been another learning experience conducted over many years: I have learnt so much from so many different people (as widely various as the late Donald Stewart and the late John P MacIntosh MP, the late Sir Robert Grieve, Professor Michael D Shaner, the late Angus MacGillvray, Winnie Ewing MEP and Muiris MacConghail) and I am conscious of the vast number of people like them who have contributed to my thinking about many things, including our country and its present hopes. Some are no longer with us, and cannot share in our present anticipation, but somewhere I am sure they are watching and hoping!

Some, of course, are still here and working. I am particularly grateful to Alex and Moira Salmond for their constant friendship and strong support over the last eleven years, although I am perhaps not so grateful for the increasing pressures that those years have brought to all of us! Those pressures rest on the shoulders of many individuals who collaborate closely and who are also, therefore, friends.

As this book is going to press Dr Allan Macartney, one of those friends, died very suddenly. It would have been good to have had his witty and wise views on what I have seen and how I have recounted my (and Muir's) story. We will all miss him.

One other individual who has contributed greatly, and shouldered much more than should have been expected of him, is Kevin Pringle. He deserves special thanks as he agreed to add to his burdens and (as a friend) read this manuscript in proof. In so doing he offered many valuable and wise suggestions. Tolerance of my need (occasionally) to do things like write books rather than always be available at my desk extends to all my other colleagues in the SNP, especially those working at SNP HQ particularly to Allison Hunter, Irene White, Alex Bell, Craig Milroy and Sam Barber and to my assistants Joan Knott and Duncan Hamilton. To all of them I give my thanks for being the best team in the business! And I must also thank a former HQ colleague, Andrew Wilson, for reading the early chapters and commenting constructively.

I am also grateful to George Bruce for his illuminating thoughts on Edwin Muir, to his son David for introducing me to his father, and to Dennis and Glynis MacLeod for constantly being thought-provoking about this country in which we live.

Finally without my family I would do nothing but I know that I have not yet learnt the balance in which I can give the time I should to them and still do all the other things I seem to be called to do, or insist on being called to do!

Thanks once more – with love – to Cathleen and Cailean.

Feorlean, Glendaruel, Argyll
September 1998

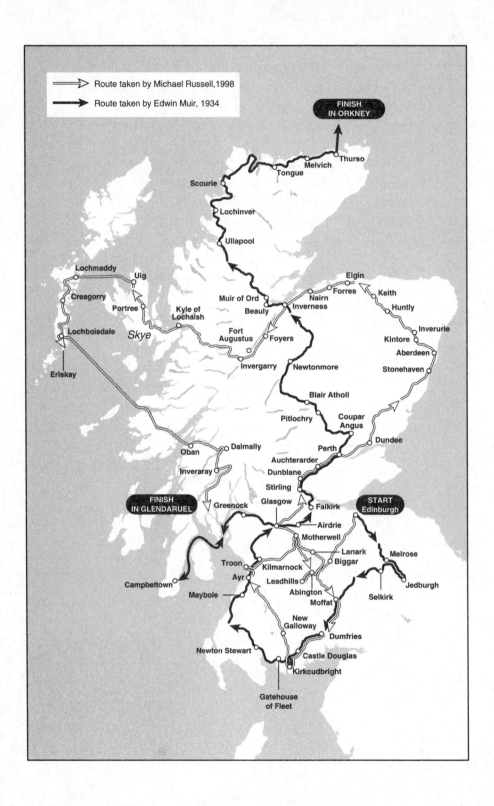

Introduction

National identity grows from the stories we tell to ourselves about ourselves.

Roderick Watson in *Scotland: A Concise Cultural History* (1993)

It has never been difficult to travel in an imaginary Scotland. From John Galt's *Dalmailing*, through George MacKay Brown's *Hamnavoe* to the *Lunderston* of Robin Jenkins there was and is a wealth of imaginary places that speak of the Scotland that we think we know, and whose homes, and streets and intrigues remind us of who we are and what we have become. And of course we must not forget our time spent in Thrums. Not least because Scotland almost got stuck in Thrums.

John Galt's parish was a place that mocked itself – and his minister, the wonderfully self-blind, socially climbing, unco guid Mr Balwhidder is a subtle portrait of great power. But Galt's sharp wit and minute dissection were not matched by others and Scottish letters at times seemed to deteriorate into a mawkish sentimentality that (like ugly brassicas) have flowered into a full cabbage patch: a kailyard.

In kailyard Scotland steam trains arrived but never left, policemen were honest and helpful and got away with the odd paternal skite of the hand across the lug of a young malefactor. Ministers, doctors and even dominies were respected and every busybody got their comeuppance from the wise, but misunderstood, mother with the heart of gold whose decency overcame the miserly Presbyterianism of her surroundings.

The honesty and self-mocking of Dalmailing, though, had not died. Its roots were deep – twining past Scott, avoiding Henry MacKenzie and thrusting towards Blind Harry, who spoke of grand things in ordinary language. In the early part of the 20th century it was – like the Scottish people themselves – merely comatose, stunned by the regular application of bagpipes, tartan (neither of which had anything to do with the lowland village of the cabbage patch) lucky white heather and the Provost's chain, bouncing on the well-satisfied corporation of the senior Baillie. And although it still takes the odd blow from the *Sunday Post* and the *People's Friend* (the last vestiges of that smell of sickly boiled cabbage) it has reasserted itself in the latter part of the 20th century with a vengeance – perhaps more than a vengeance when confronted with the grisly (but sadly hilarious) real life of Leith and Granton that is the modern Dalmailing for Irvine Welsh.

The imaginary Scotland – the tree tops of the cone gatherers, the graveyards of Old Mortality, the waterfall of the justified sinner – is still, no matter when it was created, a powerful Scotland standing apart from the fashions that from time to time have diverted it from its strongest stream. And it is a Scotland that has often allowed us to look behind our political condition to something more important – our condition as human beings, sharing a small part of the planet and making connections based on our common experiences.

The stories we tell ourselves about ourselves are usually true to the times in which we find ourselves. They are, after all, a product of those times but if they achieve timelessness – if the achieve the immortality of Dalmailing – it is not just because they are well told but because they also touch an eternal, or at least long-lasting, truth. They touch on our identity – either individual or collective and they illuminate, and perhaps improve, the way in which we live our lives.

But there is another way to learn about our lives and it involves travelling in a more difficult landscape: one that is constantly shifting and the people in it are always redefining themselves. That is a real landscape, with real people. Visiting such landscapes and people is also enshrined in a Scottish literary tradition – the tradition of Martin Martin, voyaging in the Western Isles, of Boswell trying to reconcile the irascible Johnson to the facts of 18th century life, and of Alasdair Alpin MacGregor being reviled for his views on Stornoway (such writing is an occupational hazard – it happened to John MacCulloch and Hugh Miller too). It is a tradition of travelling and telling, of Scots looking at Scotland and trying to understand who and what we are.

It is a tradition that has also, from time to time, gone wrong. Not for the chauvinistic reasons that many of the writers were not from the places they looked at – though familiarity usually helps, as does a forgiving eye – but because sometimes they were keen only on straitjacketing their observations to fit a pre-conceived notion of progress, or political correctness.

And it reaches its low point in a new genre, which does not even travel but sits at home and contemplates our country. Duncan Bruce's *The Mark of the Scots* is no doubt well meant, but exhausting in its litany of those people and things that arise out of supposed Scottish genius. By the time a Scottish ancestry has been claimed for Charles De Gaulle, the Mayor of Warsaw and Andrea Kambila – the first of the Russian boyars – it is hard not to stifle a giggle, still less a yawn. And if the Scots really did invent sea canoeing, basketball and lawn bowling then hell mend us.

I undertake this short essay on writing about Scotland deeply aware that I am likely to fall into all of the above the pitfalls myself. I am hardly an independent or unbiased observer of my own country, having spent much of the past 25 years trying to change it. I find it difficult to relate to a place or a person without filtering them through my own prejudices and experiences – and they are usually firmly held, though always subject to change. And as my profession (perhaps I should call it a trade) is, in part, to convert those who do not share my point of view, the manifesto will undoubtedly get into the picture from time to time, no matter how hard I try to hide it.

But this book is not – or at least is not meant to be – 'a nationalist on the nation'. In part my writing is an attempt to escape from the straight jacket of day to day politics and to indulge in the luxury of visiting and thinking about the country and its people, trying to learn from them what my country is about, and what it wants to be.

I first discussed the idea of this book with Neil Wilson, my ever-patient publisher, in the convivial surroundings of the Ceilidh Place in Ullapool. We were promoting my earlier book on the German film maker Werner Kissling, and I was experiencing the early days of the grind of an author's tour. Neil said yes to the idea very readily – the whiskies at the Ceilidh Place are very persuasive – but the problem of how I would actually tackle the idea took longer to be solved.

It was another Scottish publisher – Hugh Andrew – who first suggested that I read Edwin Muir's *Scottish Journey* and perhaps use it as a template for my own wandering. *Scottish Journey* is a book more talked about than read these days, but it was an illumination to me. Professor Christopher Smout said that it 'held a mirror up to the face Scotland' and went on to comment that: 'It is frightening to see so many recognisable features lingering in the glass.'

Well, up to a point Lord Copper. Smout was writing in 1979 in the post-referendum depression. Scotland in 1998 is a very different country from Scotland in 1934 or even 1979. Its relative economic prosperity is staggering compared to the desolation of the depression, but then that is true of most of Western Europe (though not of the vast majority of countries in the world). More importantly its spirit seems to have changed – it is no longer a place in danger of losing its identity, but rather a place with a bewildering range of possibilities set before it. The lion finally has roared, and is now looking through the open cage door with anticipation, though not yet with certainty. The act of choosing our future is the task of the moment, and that fact above all makes it important that somebody takes at look at the place and the people whilst we do so.

Integrating Muir into my thoughts about the book has

been more difficult. Muir has very little reported speech in his book and a great deal of reflection. At times for a modern reader the book is a bit impenetrable simply because of the slabs of text. A generation brought up on tabloid newspapers, television and comics – including even those who say they never look at such things – has a lower threshold of boredom or thought than our parents or grandparents. At the same time I am not a working journalist, with a shorthand notebook and an ability to blend in and worm the answers out of unsuspecting punters (though not all journalists do that, I accept!). Whilst I planned to talk to lots of people, in reality I found myself wanting to think more than speak and to use the unusual experience of solitude to consider what was going on around me. My time was also committed to so many other things that I could not even consider the type of leisurely journey in an open-topped car that Muir found so engaging.

So I tackled my journey in a different way with the purpose not of copying Muir, but of loosely following in his footsteps – from time to time departing from his route and as often as not seeing different things even in the same place. Muir is a companion, not a guide for my journey. And I have also dipped in and out of my travels – spending a day here, a day there and always using past visits and knowledge to supplement, influence and sometimes replace more recent impressions.

The Scotland I found I have tried to report faithfully. But I have also tried to report faithfully the thoughts about that Scotland that were occasioned by my journey and by the act of writing it all down. Of necessity that process is wide ranging and, also of necessity, I do not always come to the expected conclusion. There are things about this country that have not changed for the better, and there are dangers and pitfalls ahead that will need more than political solutions.

The title for the book was the first thing I thought of. Scotland is 'in waiting' for its parliament, and in a broader sense it is 'in waiting' too. Three centuries of being the invisible nation of Europe, as Chris Harvie put it, are coming to an end, but how or when we walk out on to the world stage is still not decided. We are in waiting in the wings of history. The curtain is about to go up. Fine as the imagined Scotland is, it is the real Scotland that will have to perform. I hope that some of that real Scotland, and some of that feeling of antici-pation, is expressed in these pages.

Chapter One
Edwin Muir's *Scottish Journey*, 1935

In the summer of 1934 the poet Edwin Muir set off from
Edinburgh in an open-top 1921 Standard car (borrowed from
his school-friend Stanley Cursister by then Director of the
Scottish National Gallery) to discover what he could about a
Scotland that he called 'a confusing conglomeration
containing such strange anachronisms as Edinburgh, a great
expanse of cultivated and a greater of fallow land and a
number of different races'. The result was *Scottish Journey*,
published in 1935 by Gollancz and reprinted in 1979 and 1996
by Mainstream. Although a span of 64 years might seem small
in relation to other events and historical eras, at the time of
writing it seems an eternity.

In the intervening years two world ideologies have risen
and fallen, Fascism and Communism. His journey was made
before computers, space flight, television and even before
AIDS and Viagra. Living in a time in which change is the
norm, even the way of life in our own country all those years
ago now seems foreign to us. Of course our vision of our past
– even our recent past – is somewhat skewed by the ability to
watch it on screen. The assumption that film gives an
immediacy to an event is only partly true: it also distances us
by the conscious and unconscious comparisons we can make

with our own time – the fashions, the ways of walking and talking, the buildings, the cars: all place an event outwith our experience, or in our past and create a barrier that, paradoxically, may not be as strong with times more distant but which we cannot view in the familiar, contemporary visual media.

1934 was the year in which the *Queen Mary* was launched. We can watch the launch in archive film and feel it represents a way of living and working and that it relates to a world that we no longer understand. Who are these people in their long coats, in their formal poses, in their working overalls? Perhaps they are our fathers and mothers and grandmothers, but they are also merely figures on a screen, figures under some distant and dimly understood sky. Muir's Scotland *is* the Scotland of 1934, a Scotland that is only just beginning, very slowly, to come out of the most profound economic depression in modern times. This was a depression that Muir had lived through, albeit in Hampstead and then St Andrews rather than in the industrial heartlands that suffered so greatly; yet it was the effects of that depression – observed 'in a mining district of Lanarkshire' – that first prompted Muir to think about his Scottish journey.

Muir's commission for the book came from Heinemann and Gollancz, who had already produced *English Journey* by JB Priestley. The advance he received he intended to use to pay for a holiday in Orkney for his family – his five-year-old son was still recovering from the serious effects of a road accident in 1933. Muir's choice of Orkney for his family's recovery reflected his idealistic view of the place where he was born in 1887. 'I'm not Scotch', he said in a letter in 1926, 'I'm an Orkney man, a good Scandinavian and my country is Norway or Denmark or Iceland or some place like that.' But he wisely added 'This is nonsense, I am afraid, though there's some sense in it'. And later in *Scottish Journey* he describes living in Orkney as 'the only desirable form of life that I found in all my journey through Scotland'.

Muir lived that life (on the island of Wyre) until the age of fourteen when his family moved to Glasgow so that his father – a failed tenant farmer at a time when agricultural change was even affecting distant, perfect Orkney – could find work. Within a year of arriving in the city – a city which Muir found frightening and dirty – his father had died of a heart attack. A year later one of his brothers had contracted fatal consumption and shortly afterwards another brother and his mother also died. At eighteen he was effectively alone in an alien environment.

Muir survived in that environment until 1919 when he married and moved south. His day to day work included two years as a bookkeeper in a bone factory in Greenock, working in an office reeking of decay to the sound of a fellow employee shooting seagulls outside to keep them off the maggots that teemed on the rotting flesh piled up in the yard. The experience features in *Scottish Journey*, described in the third person, and concludes with the very moving description of the effect of his workplace upon his fellow workers – and by extension the effect of all demeaning work upon those whose lives are bound up in it:

Edwin Muir's *Scottish Journey*, 1935

3

> *He had heard that the men and women who worked in the yard, unloading the bones and casting them in the furnace never got rid of the smell, no matter how they scrubbed. It got among the women's hair and in the pores of their skin. They breathed it into the faces of their lovers when at night under the hawthorn bushes outside the town they found a few moments sensual forgetfulness: they breathed it out with the last breath, infecting the Host which the priest set between their lips...*

It is obvious that Muir never got over his Glasgow and Greenock experiences – the chapter on Glasgow in *Scottish Journey* is the longest in the book and full of criticism and dislike. And yet Muir saved himself from total breakdown at this crucial time in his life by espousing that thing which has been so important in changing Glasgow – socialism. And by espousing socialism he could move his individual dislikes and disasters into the purposeful straitjacket of an ideology.

Yet Muir has been described as a politician who disliked political parties, and a Christian who never went to Church. The poet George Bruce describes him as a man 'who recognised the necessity of politics, but didn't operate in the political world at all'. Certainly there is little active support in *Scottish Journey* for the Labour Party (and still less of an account of the work his party was doing and had done for industrial Scotland) but there is much criticism of the nascent SNP, although he agreed strongly with their aim of self-government. Religion is also not to the fore in *Scottish Journey*, although it was an abiding issue in Scotland then as it is now.

Before his marriage to the brilliant, outgoing effervescent Willa Anderson – who was much more concerned with the realities of the world than he was – and their move in 1919 Muir had become involved first of all in the Independent Labour Party, and then in Socialist publications like *The New Age*, a London-based vehicle for intellectual middle-class socialists run by a self-educated Yorkshireman, AR Orage, who became a close friend and patron to Muir. But because Muir was an outsider – a bookkeeper and clerk rather than a shipyard worker or labourer, a writer rather than an activist – it was his reaction to the circumstances of industrial Scotland and to its decay with all the human problems that were caused in the depression, which provided the underlying theme of *Scottish Journey*.

This element of an 'outsider's view' is confirmed in one of the most outstanding tributes made to Muir after his death. TS Eliot provided the introduction to the Faber 1965 edition of Muir's selected poems – a posthumous introduction for Eliot as well as Muir, as it turned out, for although it was recorded for the BBC Third Programme, as an appreciation of Muir's work, it was only published after Eliot's own death too.

In it, Eliot calls Muir 'one of the poets of whom Scotland should always be proud'. But he goes onto comment that 'there is something essential (in Muir) which is neither English or Scottish, but Orcadian. There is the sensibility of the remote islander, the boy from a primitive offshore community who then was plunged into the sordid horror of industrialism in Glasgow, who struggled to understand the modern world of the metropolis'.

Understanding the modern world was something that Muir was trying to do from his earliest writings. In 1918 (under the pseudonym Edward Moore) he had published a book actually called *We Moderns* which leaned heavily on his reading of Nietzsche rather than on Marx. The following year Willa resigned her teaching job to go with him to London where he wrote for Orage and took a variety of menial jobs while she supported him by taking school posts. Both of them were delighted, however, with the socialist, intellectual and self-styled 'modern' company in which they found themselves.

Muir took sessions of psychotherapy and started an interest in dreams and imagination – he also succeeded in selling articles to the American journal *The Freeman* and with an increase in his journalistic earnings the couple decided to move to the Continent where the money went even further. Muir and Willa settled in Prague at first – he was overwhelmed by the beauty of the city – and then moved to Hellerau near Dresden. This started a process of wandering, during which they would live for a while in whatever place took their fancy – including the then obscure small town of St Tropez. Muir called this period one of 're-discovery and awakening' and it seems to have healed the scars of Glasgow and the bone factory – and those aspects of capitalism against which he had railed but which had wounded him so greatly. Muir earned his living by translating, reviewing and writing and he had published a number of books during the 1920s including two of criticism, and three novels, as well as his first book of poetry, *First Poems* in 1925.

The Muirs had a son, Gavin, born in 1927 and they then returned to Britain, where his reputation as a critic and as a translator – working with Willa – grew apace and resulted in highly successful translations of Kafka and Hermann Broch.

Several of his Scottish friends tried to interest him in returning to Scotland and in 1932 the Scottish Branch of Pen International persuaded him to visit again, as part of their plan to tempt back Scottish writers to Scotland. In 1933 the family had a holiday in Orkney and Muir conceived of *Scottish Journey* as he drove through the mining districts of Lanarkshire. In 1934 he attended the PEN Conference held in the Church of Scotland Assembly Hall in Edinburgh. With the commission for *Scottish Journey* already agreed, he set out in his borrowed car immediately after the conference, sending Willa and Gavin ahead to Orkney.

Muir's *Scottish Journey* – a Scottish journey, not *The* Scottish journey, as Muir reminds his readers in his preface, 'not a survey, but a bundle of impressions' – was written some months after the journey, in the early part of 1935 when Muir had returned to London and before he moved to St Andrews. He was 48 when it appeared, and it was not particularly well received – he himself does not refer to it in his later autobio-graphical work, *The Story and the Fable*, published in 1940, nor even in his fuller *An Autobiography* published in 1954, and Willa only gives it a brief glance in her memoir about her life with Edwin Muir *Belonging* published in 1968. His further attempt to say something about his native land – *Scott on Scotland* – which was published a year later was more noticed, but also a source of much controversy as Muir argued that writing in Scots was futile.

Scottish Journey is, at times, an angry book, and Scotland had much to be angry about in 1934. Though social conditions had improved considerably since the start of the century – mobility, trade union activism and the election of the first Labour government had all contributed to such progress – the depression precipitated, or at least signalled, by the Wall Street Crash of October 1929 had bitten very hard into the country. By 1933 the Clyde shipyards were producing less than ten percent of their 1913 output; Scottish coal mines were employing about half of the pre-First World War number of miners and the Scottish steel industry's share of UK production had been cut by 50 percent. The Borders woollen mills were all on part-time working, Dundee jute production was virtually at a standstill and in rural Scotland the exodus from the country to the cities – an exodus with no promised land at the end of it – had accelerated as a result of falling agricultural prices and a collapse in fishing.

The Scottish population fell during the depression – the first fall since the start of the decennial census – with net migration from the country mirroring the flight from country to town. But jobs were no easier to get furth of the country – the raw figures of 20% unemployment in the UK as a whole, compared to the 26% for Scotland gave few emigrants to the South any real hope whilst high American and Canadian unemployment closed off a traditional route to a better life.

In crude summary Muir's *Scottish Journey* not only arises out of this social catastrophe but also tries to analyse its causes and possible solutions. This is a crude summary because the book is much more discursive than this, but there is no doubt that the plight of his country aroused both his concern and his anger. And that plight raised in his mind the whole question of Scottish identity and its survival. Again and again he comments on the 'idle' population – mostly male. The street corners of Airdrie and Motherwell – but also of Dumfries and other places in rural Scotland – were full of men with nothing to do, and for whom, as he puts it, there is 'nowhere else to go and little prospect that Monday will dawn for a long time'.

But his opinions were also coloured by what he believed was an inability of Scots to address the many and pressing problems of their nation. Attracted to the idea of self-government (though anti-Nationalist in the sense of the party politics of his time, he had been the driving force behind the establishment of a Scottish centre for PEN and the successful claim for a separate Scottish representation in that organisation), he saw the biggest barrier to change in the apathy of both the people and their representatives. His remedy for this was political, but only in the sense that political debate about the future might 'quicken national life and bring about an

Edwin Muir's
Scottish Journey,
1935

7

internal regeneration', although he expected the process to be slow and without certainty of success. 'The great mass of the population', he claimed, 'are still sunk in indifference and this acceptance of the sordid third or fourth best, imported from every side, is what oppresses one so much as one walks down the streets'.

Muir had been disillusioned by the right-wing backlash to the depression and to the formation of a National Government in 1931, which had resulted in the return of only seven Labour MPs in Scotland (compared to 38 at the 1929 General Election). However Labour was far from done in Scotland, with 24 Labour and ILP MPs elected in 1935, two years after Labour gained control of Glasgow at the municipal election – a control that has lasted with only slight interruptions ever since. In this period of political, social and economic crisis Muir saw indifference everywhere: in the upper and middle classes in Edinburgh conducting their lives with no knowledge of what had shaped their society, and therefore having neither the ability or the curiosity to change things: in the whole population of Glasgow and West Central Scotland who were guilty of a 'deliberate blunting of one whole area of their sensibility', so that they would not have to confront the grimness of their lives and surroundings: in both the customers and staff of a Highland inn where he stayed on his journey: everywhere indeed except in his beloved Orkney from whence he had been torn as a child and which formed the grail of the book's quest.

It is significant that the first modern edition of Muir's *Scottish Journey* was published in 1979 and that many commentators saw strong parallels between the failings of that year (the end of a political generation) and Muir's observations and conclusions. For example industrial Lanarkshire, (the 19th-century talisman of success and enterprise) was declining fast with nothing to replace this engine of the economy. And to add insult to injury the detritus of the Industrial Revolution had turned gold into dross, and created a landscape that was still blighted by the 'pocked fields through which iron-coloured brooks sluggishly oozed'. Muir shuddered at this landscape covered with towns and villages that lay 'jumbled together in a wilderness of grime, coal dust and brick, under a blackish-grey synthetic sky'.

And plenty of journalists and writers were asking in 1979 the plaintive question that Muir asked of the nascent SNP in 1934: 'Where is the force that will drive the people of Scotland to proclaim themselves a nation?', and answering it with the same sort of words: 'In the heads of a few people, mainly middle class ...but meanwhile the people themselves ...are being driven by the logic of economic necessity to a quite different end.'

Muir's grasp of economics, of course, was not of the first order. He wrote a pamphlet in 1935 entitled *Social Credit and the Labour Party* which espoused the chaotic and unworkable theories of Major CG Douglas – theories that are still being peddled by a few in Scotland despite the fact that their origins lie not in the world of figures and facts, but in the desire to find a third way between the 1930's failure of democratic socialism, (Ramsay MacDonald-style), and the harsh communism of Stalin that was beginning to emerge. But Muir did understand poverty and its effects – not just from his childhood, but also because of his own financial difficulties from time to time as he struggled to make his way. And he raged against the effects of such poverty in his own country .

Edwin Muir's *Scottish Journey*, 1935

9

He also raged against – though the language is different, and the tone one of despair rather than determination – the decline of Scottish identity and tied this up to the economic and social problems he saw around him – and to their origins. His 'main impression' to which he draws attention in the introduction to *Scottish Journey* is that 'Scotland is gradually being emptied of its population, its spirit, its wealth, industry, art, intellect and innate character...If a country exports its most enterprising spirits and best minds year after year, for fifty or a hundred or two hundred years, some result will inevitably follow...no civilization that is composed merely of exploiters and exploited can endure for long.'

Muir also called Scotland 'a land lost to history', forgetful of its past and indifferent to its future. He expected the country to continue to export its best minds and to be emptied of creativity and renewal – to be incapable of that rediscovery which had been an important part of his personal voyage. Yet at the very time he was writing, Scotland was undergoing a literary renaissance – one that he was a part of, and wrote about. And contemporaneously with his writing about Scotland, Scottish historians were beginning to analyse and explore our past so that his assertion that 'all Scottish history is inadequate and confusing: it has still to be written', would shortly become an anachronism itself. Scottish history continues to attract new talents and new interest – it has been progressively both popularised and then subject to revisionism. Today we stand on the threshold of the opening of a major new museum of the Scottish past, which will draw even more people towards an understanding of who we are and where we came from.

Some parts of Muir's observations are dated and no longer relevant: some parts are chillingly familiar, as Chris Smout points out in his introductions to both the 1979 and 1996 editions of *Scottish Journey*. But overall the book serves two important purposes – it expresses much about our country that we need to know, if only to mark how we have changed, and how much we still need to change. It also provides a valuable source for a study of 1930's social and political attitudes – a study of a time when socialism still meant the building of a new Jerusalem, and when (to quote from Smout in his comparison with 1979) Labour had no vision except the retention of power, when the Conservatives knew exactly how to play on the people's fear of change and when the Nationalists had no 'clear or noble social purpose'.

Smout claims that 1979 was the same sort of time. A time of a 'lethargic and divided people, quick to resent a trifling insult but incapable of action to remedy their plight.' He may well be right, not least because in 1979 Scotland inflicted on itself a classic Caledonian own goal and snatched defeat from the jaws of victory in a democratic debacle the ghost of which was only laid to rest in 1997.

But time has moved on. Muir's Scotland is not today's Scotland – though there may be the odd remnant of what Muir saw still lurking in parts of our country. This is a country that for the first time since 1707 has a chance to remedy its own ills, and to build its own future. Or it may even be that our chance of a new future has been created by a process of change that was already starting in Muir's time, a process of historical development which happened to be depicted by Muir only at one of its lower ebbs. Muir's Scotland of 1934 may have been a shadow Scotland only because of the age that he happened to live in.

It is time to find all that out. To make another Scottish Journey.

Edwin Muir's
Scottish Journey,
1935

11

Chapter Two
Edinburgh

On a raw, wet, winter's day – say at around eleven in the morning, at the bottom of the Royal Mile – it is possible to believe Tom Stoppard's memorable jibe at Edinburgh as the 'Reykjavik of the South'. This slight is somewhat ungrateful, considering that Stoppard's reputation and fortune were made by the success of his first play *Roseancrantz and Guildenstern are Dead* on the Edinburgh Festival Fringe.

It is such a day today, a day soon after the undistinguished, faded 50s' office block alongside a disused brewery site has been designated the home in waiting of Scotland's parliament. Where better to start the search for Scotland's first parliament in 300 years than at the actual place where it will come into being...the blank sheet of paper, so to speak, on which it will be written. So I have come here as a sort of advance guard, the first pilgrim to the shrine of Scottish Democracy. Appropriately there is really nothing to see.

But no matter where I stand to look at this place I am still conscious of the looming backdrop of Calton Hill behind. There is already a parliamentary chamber in waiting up there and a five-minute walk up the Canongate would reveal the original Parliament House next to St Giles Cathedral. Having been denied its democratic heart for so long Scotland now has three pretenders to the vacant cavity. There is something archetypically Scottish about this situation. With thrawn determination, the government that Scots have been voting for throughout the Thatcher years and which has now 'come up with the goods', has chosen the wrong option.

But not everybody thinks so, of course. The publicans of the bottom end of the High Street are in raptures (although rapture perhaps sits ill on a Scottish landlord – quiet anticipation of profit would be a better term) and a Scottish hotel company is delirious. Its adjacent site has literally won the jackpot with the prospect of eternal business from the elected, the hopeful and the wage slaves who are going to be hereabouts within a few years. And for those who want to play down Scottish aspirations for self-government, it seems only right to hide the parliament away 'over the back', barely visible except from Salisbury Crags, and almost inaccessible by public transport.

But that is not entirely fair. Apparently there will be new roads opened up, trams re-established and even a car park (civic Edinburgh in its present incarnation hates the car in the way that the Inquisition hated heretics.) And whatever appears will not just be the product of flawed and politically timid decision making, but also of the best hopes, talents and aspirations of the most ambitious architects in the world

It is also encouraging that the successful design for the parliament will be chosen not just by the same crew who decided upon the site, but also by some people who actually believe in the project. Broadcaster Kirsty Wark, one of the members of the selection panel, persuaded me of that over a drink after one of her programmes, talking with excitement and enthusiasm about shape, light and access whilst managing to evade a junior Scottish Office minister who was attempting to persuade her that the House of Lords debating chamber had the best proportions for debate in the world, and should therefore form the holy of holies in the new building.

The views of the parliament's neighbour in the palace on what should be built next to her are not known, although planning law usually allows residents in the vicinity an opinion on the matter. Holyroodhouse is reputed to be the Queen's least favourite residence: draughty, dingy and entirely ceremonial. Douglas Hurd's fictional monarch in *Scotch on the Rocks* balks at spending three months a year there, even though his presence would save the Union, and complains of the cold rooms and the smell from the brewery. The bloodstain on the floor where Rizzio died is supposed to be visible but any attempt to view it seems to be blocked by quixotic opening hours. The closest I have been – 25 years ago – was as a guest by lottery at the annual garden party for the Church of Scotland General Assembly, which is a cold and tedious way of acquiring a free fish-paste sandwich and a tepid cup of tea. I didn't see the Queen, but the movement of the crowd at a particular moment indicated she was there much in the way that shoals of pilot fish reveal the presence of a whale.

I should declare an interest both in the parliament and in Edinburgh. As I start my search for what it is that Scotland expects or desires from its new institution, I am on home ground. In the way that some people spend their lives hoping that their football team will win the Cup, I have spent the last quarter of a century waiting for a parliament. Not this parliament, admittedly, although we were all gradualists in the 1970s, new recruits to a party that seemed to have got so far so fast that our goal was anything that might be achieved quickly. But as this parliament is the best that is coming along this year, or next year – barring a political earthquake – then this is the parliament that we should welcome, and build upon and allow to grow.

And I am on home turf of a type too in Edinburgh. My mother was brought up in the city, and as a child I visited grandparents who seem in retrospect amazingly exotic, as though they were the final flowering of another age and lifestyle. I was at university here; I worked here and came back regularly when I was living and working elsewhere. And then in 1994 I took the post of Chief Executive of the SNP and so returned to work again, travelling as regularly as I could between Edinburgh and the west, where I left my wife and son as I followed the grail of the parliament once more.

We wear our past close to our skin, sometimes vaguely itchy, sometimes completely unfelt and sometimes all too invasive as it pushes in on us, demanding our attention. And because Edinburgh holds so much of my past, a day in the city with nothing to do but think about it and meander through it, has a special attraction. Today I am starting my voyage of discovery so I decide to follow my instincts and turn up the Canongate to walk up the Royal Mile, with half an intent to visit the Castle, knowing full well that I shall probably put that off for another day – as I have done since my last visit at the age of 11.

I lie. It was not quite my last visit. In the summer of 1997, with the triumphalism of victory, New Labour hosted a reception for the centenary of the STUC in the Great Hall of the castle. I was about the only person present who was not either a member of the party, or who did not claim in a stage whisper to be delighted about the landslide (and claim to be part of it). After the speeches the Secretary of State ordered the Honours of Scotland to be unlocked, and the guests were invited to see the Stone of Scone – returned some months earlier after 700 years in England (give or take a few weeks around Christmas 1950 when Ian Hamilton and his friends played their great prank).

I was one of the few who took the time to tramp through the exhibition, conscious that I had never seen it before. The displays were unexpectedly cramped and the story of the discovery of the honours by Sir Walter Scott was more impressive than the jewels themselves. The Stone though, was the greatest disappointment of all. It is hard to get excited by a lump of sedimentary rock, and harder still when all probability suggests that it is not Jacob's pillow, the *Lia Faill* which was brought out of ancient Ireland, but some sort of mediaeval substitute, cobbled together by monks to deceive a looting, raping and rampaging army. I stood for a long while beside its glass case but there was no buzz from it, and no

feeling of mystic significance. I was glad it was there all right –
it seemed only right that stolen property should be returned –
but the case for change in Scotland is infinitely more
substantial than that represented by a quasi-Celtic relic. I went
back to the reception and had another drink.

Edinburgh is not a city for umbrellas – the snell wind from
the Firth of Forth can turn them inside out whenever you go
round a corner – so I shrug off the damp air that passes for rain
and beat my way up the High Street, passing the knick-knack
shops, the small galleries, the coffee shops, the museums and
the other detritus of tourism. I pass an odd gaggle of
Americans, seemingly dressed as extras for *Captains
Courageous*, one even with a sou'wester jammed onto his head.
No Edinburgher would be seen giving in to the elements in
that way.

The bottom end of the High Street is not my favourite part
of Edinburgh. It holds itself together almost fearfully, narrow
and cramped and bleeding off on both sides to what even 20
years ago were slums. Once past the bottleneck of the
Netherbow (where the gate to the city once stood) the Royal
Mile is revealed in all its glory – forward towards the spaciousness of St Giles and Old Parliament Square and back down the
hill to the dark cloisters and environs of Holyroodhouse.

Edinburgh is a city of such contrasts: 'Extraordinary and
sordid', Muir called them, perhaps a little sourly: top and
bottom of the Royal Mile, Old Town and New Town, affluent
suburbs and poverty-stricken housing estates, the Pentland
Hills and the sea shore at Silverknowes, the old Roman port of
Cramond and the massive power station at Cockenzie, even
the old joke of 'fur coats and nae knickers' and the claim of
Edinburgh's most celebrated brothel keeper, the late Dora
Noyes, that her busiest time of year was during the sitting of
the General Assembly of the Church of Scotland! Edinburgh,
the Jekyll and Hyde city, where John Knox preached sermons
and ogled young girls; the birthplace of a form of Calvinism in
which pre-destination both secured a place in heaven and
allowed total licence in mortal life.

Up the street I spy the pub named after the infamous Deacon Brodie, respectable by day and criminal by night. Contrasts, contrasts. I recall Princes Street on a night last summer, when I was working late during the referendum and was searching for a bus home. As the pubs and clubs emptied, this most spectacular of European thoroughfares became a mass of drunken teenagers from Pilton and Craigmillar, staggering for taxis and screaming for fish suppers.

I am thinking about this when I get bumped by a tourist who then interrogates me about the location of the Castle. It is time to get off the winter streets. I put off my visit to the castle (I knew I would) and dip down by the court, taking the long stairs to Princes Street, partly to catch a glimpse again of the Forth and the hills of Fife beyond. Cities which you can see out of are big enough for me and when I can't see out of them – in London particularly – I want to get out as fast as possible.

I also want to talk to somebody and start enquiring about Scotland's future and its parliament. Two youths are sitting on the wall at the bottom of the steps and I try an opening line – something about what they want for the future. They look at me as if I am mad – not bampot mad, but undercover, threatening, busybody mad. One of them tells me to fuck off when the other remarks, quite quietly, that it's time Scotland ran itself. 'Time for a change, pal. We cannae do worse.'

Billy and John are from Pilton. They don't work but would like to. They are both about 17, well out of school (in fact and in attitude) and 'well rid o' it'. They want something to happen, but in the general, not the particular. And they don't have much hope that it will make their own lives better. In fact that idea doesn't even seem to register. It will be better in the way that the world will be better when the Jam Tarts win the league. No more or no less.

Our exchange is quickly exhausted. Billy has the edgy look of someone who is in need of artificial stimulation, and knows where to get it. I give the all-purpose Scots 'Aye' and leave them there. Not exactly representative, but illuminating none the less. Or at least a start in the process of asking questions and getting answers. I am on a bit of a high myself, having had to steel myself to the task of sampling opinion. It's fine when you've got a clipboard and a canvass sheet – but I'm not selling anything, or trying to get anybody's vote. I simply want to find out what is happening and if we can get there (wherever 'there' is) from here.

I am wondering if I could cope with the 'repressed sexuality' that Muir claims to have found in the tearoom in Jenner's (though when I used to visit with grandmother in the late 50s it only redolated face powder, expensive perfume and women who seemed impossibly old) when I turn to look back at the Castle and am reminded of Muir's description. 'A city built upon rock and guarded by rock'. And of his affection for both Princes Street with its 'spacious gardens and single line of buildings' and the New Town in which 'everything breathes spaciousness, order and good sense; the houses present a dignified front to the world; they suggest comfortable privacy and are big enough for large parties, and seem admirably planned to withstand the distractions and allow the amenities of rational city life'.

Muir went on to claim that the existence of this paragon of civic planning shows that 'a hundred years ago Edinburgh possessed a boldness of foresight and a standard of achievement which at that time were remarkable'. They seem even more remarkable today, confronted with one of the grandest streets in the world which is now a rickle of plate glass-windowed chain stores and novelty shops, and to which crowds flock to gawp at jeans, silk flowers, fashion shoes and remaindered books. Above their heads are the jutting concrete lintels that testify to another plan of boldness and foresight – the first-floor walkway – which was conceived and thrown away within a space of ten years and which was the last great chance to develop this street in keeping with the grandeur of its setting.

Edinburgh's elected council have had more ideas about the future of this city centre than most people have had hot dinners – but the best of them have never been implemented whilst the worst have hovered around threateningly for years. The *Scotsman* – Edinburgh's broadsheet still despite its national circulation – frequently publishes 'planners' drawings' envisioning a bright new future for some part of the city centre or other. These anodyne, pastel illustrations have a few androgynous people, a few cast-iron seats and vague backdrops that suggest elegance and modernity. But when tiny parts of these grand plans are implemented – and only tiny parts every seem to be implemented – the vision seems to boil down to not much more than bus lanes, traffic calming and the zig-zagging of colours on the roadway that confuse every motorist entering the city.

Edinburgh's failure to get to grips with its future – its obsession with wrong-headed ideas that are pursued with extreme vigour and then allowed to disappear without trace – has its roots not in political differences, but in a malaise that was part of Scotland long before Muir commented upon it. Scotland's economic and cultural depression after the Union of 1707 lasted for over half a century. But for the century after that it made the best of its situation, sublimating the talents that would have gone into governance with an eruption of creativity and commerce. Nineteenth-century Scotland reconciled itself to the Union, and determined to make it work. Scots participated as fully as anyone in the project of Empire and created their own niche in the services vital to the success of Britain – the army, trade and administration – while building their own institutions into bulwarks of their distinctive position as partner in a new state.

But inevitably when the dream decayed – when the long decline of Britishness started – those who embraced it for pragmatic reasons came to suffer materially and psychologically. The sensible choice would have been to work harder to restore the purpose of all the effort – a flourishing, united, prosperous and world-class nation that embraced the sum of its parts – or to change radically and seek an independent place in the world again. But the first choice depended too

much on the efforts of others who were revealing themselves
not as partners, but rather as masters on the wheel of history.
The second choice became a goal too hard to reach and too
uncertain in its outcome.

So it became easier not to choose – in fact inevitable that
no choice was made, and the status quo of the gradual slide
away from achievement became endemic in the twentieth
century. The power to do things was abrogated, and those with
energy and enthusiasm either departed for foreign shores and
a better context, or stayed and sought influential positions
closer to the still active centre. It is, after all, the provinces of
the body that die first.

So Edinburgh was no more capable of answering the
question of what to do with the growing number of gap sites,
than Glasgow was of wiping its slums from the map; or rather,
just as capable, providing the nation began to wake again, and
a choice began to emerge. The process of recreating Scotland
has been going on for 30 or more years, and the roots of our
present time of change lie further back than most nationalists
like to think. Political change has been the most sluggish part
of the whole exercise, but the energy to make such change has
grown out of a fundamental re-positioning of ourselves and
our place in the world that emerged almost without notice,
and certainly without conscious decision. Perhaps it has come
about simply because new generations became more and more
tired of more and more decline – hope deferred maketh the
heart grow sick, as the Book of Proverbs has it. But succeeding
generations are unlikely to live with that condition forever, if
it can be changed. Hope, like a dammed river, will find a way
through. But it has also come about, or at least been pushed
along, by the work and agitation of the early home rulers.

Progress in Scotland to realise the abilities and achievements of the nineteenth century has been patchy and slow.
But progress, founded on the rediscovery of Scotland, there
has been, though not without mistakes and false starts. One of
the most celebrated mistakes lurks at the east end of Princes
Street, where the St James Centre sits beneath a monstrous

concrete hotel, a car park and what was – for a comparatively brief time – the modern home of those who govern Scotland, New St Andrew's House. It also lies at the gateway to what should have been the most magnificent parliamentary quarter in Europe – an elongated rectangle that, paved and decorated, could have led the way up to the old Royal High School, faced by a stunning panorama sweeping from the Firth of Forth across the industrial east of Edinburgh, taking in the Crags, Arthur's Seat, the Old Town and the Castle with the Pentland Hills beyond. It could also have incorporated the old Post Office and the original St Andrew's House, built on the site of a jail and monumental in its solidity.

Precisely why this site should have become, in the fearful words of a government minister, a 'nationalist shibboleth', is not clear. The parliament that should have met on the hill in the early 1980s, after the last referendum, was a puny affair that – from what we know now – might have settled the constitutional question for 50 years, because the pressure for change, at that stage still not overwhelming, might have been assuaged at least temporarily.

No nationalist has ever felt warm towards what happens inside St Andrew's House itself, and indeed some have even camped outside its brooding walls in protest for weekends or – in the case of the democracy campaigners and their vigil – for 1,979 nights. You cannot see from this side of the hill a single council ward or parliamentary seat that has ever returned an elected SNP representative and one's eye is constantly drawn to the biggest Union Flag in the world, waving like some awful mutant tablecloth over the Castle.

Perhaps it is because there is so much history in the view, and so much hope deferred in the building. Or perhaps because, during the early Thatcher years and after the 1979 debacle anything that called itself, and might be suitable to become, a parliament gained an almost mystical significance. Whatever the reasons, the fondness for the site was, and is, shared by many throughout the country. Protests at its rejection have come from surprising quarters, not least those who might have been most disrupted by its choice. The inhabitants of grand and leafy Regent Terrace, including some overseas consuls, privately expressed astonishment that the best option had been rejected, and the least suitable trumpeted as a triumph of foresight.

It is a Scottish virtue – though not the most endearing – to make the best of things, so I turn away from the side of the chilly hill that I have wandered up to, grab a passing taxi and proceed on my day of freedom to rediscover the nation's capital. I am bound next for the 'Victorian, Edwardian and Neo-Georgian suburbs' – in Muir's words – 'most of them, and the last more particularly, shapeless and graceless'.

But not all of them. Down at Goldenacre – Edinburgh has a way with names – I alight to walk back up towards the site of my grandfather's printing works and the Royal Botanical Gardens. I detour into Inverleith Place to glance at a substantial sandstone corner house behind a big hedge where my maternal grandparents finally settled, having hopped all over the city after they arrived in the 1920s from Abbots Langley, near Watford. I suspect my grandfather would have reacted with astonishment to any question about a Scottish parliament. I think of him as a Tory, but in fact he was apparently an 'old fashioned Liberal' – a description my mother adhered to about her politics until the 1997 General Election when, as a voter in a key SNP marginal, she was persuaded to support Alasdair Morgan and became inordinately proud of the fact that she had helped to return an SNP MP. She even joined the party at the age of 77, making her politically risqué amongst the county Tory coffee set in douce Kirkcudbright.

Liberalism always espoused a measure of Home Rule, but to my grandfather it would have seemed ridiculous to treat such a sentiment as a political priority. What was good for business and profit was good for the country, and democracy was valuable in that regard only. His 'liberalism' was free trade and a measure of appropriate compassion for widows and orphans, who could be taken care of by charitable donation.

A large, cigar smoking, fleshy man, he drove a well-polished Bentley about the streets of Edinburgh, regularly winding the window down to berate other drivers of smaller vehicles about their carelessness. I clearly recall sitting beside him at the age of nine or ten as he roared 'When did you pass your test?' to an offending motorist who had presumed to cut in front of him in Causewayside. The question became more pertinent to him shortly afterwards when he became an early casualty of the drink-driving laws and had to resort to a somewhat less flashy Rover, albeit with a chauffeur, a retired employee who could pander to his moods.

Those moods were impressive and his tour de force was the haranguing of headwaiters and hotel staff over trivial, and usually imagined, slights to his status. Meals out with him (which were a regular occurrence when we visited) always involved complaints, summoning of managers, moving of tables and sending back of food. All of them, in my memory, come together whenever I visit the Caledonian Hotel in Edinburgh, or the Hawes Inn in South Queensferry – the latter a favourite destination during the building of the Forth Road Bridge with which he had a fascination, borne of 40 years crossing the Firth in a ferry, and waiting for hours in the queues. A table moved from the dining room to the front window of the lounge would always be ordered so that he could see the sides of the bridge creep together, and always it would either not be there, or in the wrong place. Difficult as I can be I very rarely complain when dining out – the wounds of embarrassment as a child have taken a long time to heal.

The Caledonian was memorable for other reasons too. My parents had their wedding reception there, with Lothian Road closed off momentarily as they crossed over in procession from St John's Episcopal Church at the end of Princes Street, while the Chief Constable of Edinburgh sat at my grandparents' house with a bottle of whisky, looking after the wedding presents as a favour for friends! My aunt would occasionally take up residence in the Caley, during one of her alcoholic binges when living with her parents became intolerable.

Grandfather would insist on eating there at those times, and expect her to join us. As children we would go up to her room to fetch her, watch her down a quadruple gin before descending to dine with us in a growing stupor with less and less control of what she said and did.

Aunt Dorothy was academically brilliant and personally chaotic. Oppressed from childhood, she had married a carbon paper salesman in desperation, only to give up on him within days. 'Men' – by implication unsuitable, financially predatory and always hovering around her in bars – would be mentioned darkly from time to time, but she seemed to do nothing but go out sober(ish) and return drunk to stagger to her room. As my grandparents aged she would talk about how free she would be once they were dead, with the money to do whatever she wanted (not that she was kept short of it by my grandfather's impulsive generosity to all around him). She died, of course, before my grandfather's will was even proved, succumbing to the self-inflicted triple whammy of jaundice, cirrhosis and lung cancer.

My grandmother lived much longer, dying in a nursing home in England in her mid 90s. She was of Scottish descent, her own grandfather being from Maybole in Ayrshire and from an army family. She had been beautiful at one time, but marriage to a man of strong will, who sailed close to the wind in personal and financial matters, had robbed her of any personality she had. It was rumoured that one occasion she had rebelled and left her husband, moving to London and setting herself up on his money in an expensive service flat where she subsisted on sandwiches from Fortnum and Mason. But that act of self-assertion seems to have exhausted her – she soon came back and did absolutely nothing for the rest of her life. She always had a cook and a cleaner, and latterly a personal nurse and companion (or rather a succession of them with ready access to the bottle and an ability to spot an easy life when they saw it). As long as everything was done for her she didn't fret or worry – but when she had to do something herself she erected enormous obstacles which made it impossible.

Whilst grandfather made a fortune on the black market during the war, she did nothing until, prompted to contribute to the war effort, she agreed to meet troops arriving on leave at the station, and offer tea and cigarettes to them. Typically she set out with good intentions, only to return in a taxi after an hour, having gone to the wrong station. More incredibly she failed to attend my grandfather's funeral, pleading a cold and an appointment with the chiropodist.

My mother's father owned most of two printing and publishing companies – Morrison and Gibb at Tanfield, a two-minute walk from Inverleith Place (not that I ever remember him walking) and W&AK Johnstone on the south side. Tanfield printed not only books but also bank notes for the Bank of Scotland and the Scottish Edition of the *Daily Mail*. Johnstones were map makers; their clan maps of Scotland still hang on the walls of many old schoolrooms. I can remember being surrounded by books in my grandfather's dark, wood-panelled office and one of the best pictures of him still sits on my mother's bookshelf – Fred Haynes with open book in hand, glaring at the camera.

Although he spent a week in London every month – in the Waldorf of course – his bread and butter publications were Scottish and he seemed particularly interested in Scottish reference works on the clans and septs, and military histories. But I cannot recall ever seeing him reading a book, still less a Scottish book. His sole foray into the world of ideas was his devotion to the Archers, for which dinner and conversation had to stop at 6.15 every evening.

Although based in Edinburgh, the more I think of him the more I think he could have been living in any provincial city in Britain without experiencing any great or inconvenient change in his lifestyle. He was in Edinburgh because it was – at that time – still a publishing centre of importance and because the business opportunity he came for was based there. He undoubtedly saw himself as British first and English a very close second, although he did not fall into the trap of suspecting, as is now often the case south of the Border, that the two terms are equivalent. It is almost unbelievable to me that he actually stood whenever the national anthem was played, even at home listening to the radio – and made us all stand too – and that the highlight of his Christmas was the Queen's message to the Commonwealth.

My mother though had a very Edinburgh education at Mary Erskine's and acquired the Scottish middle-class ability to blend the best of British with the best of Scottish. Edinburgh could fool itself that it mattered in the British scheme of things and provided a home for the monarch when he, and later she, deigned to cross the border. There was a semblance of power in the presence of the Secretary of State for Scotland, and a conceit that the financial and legal muscle of the city made it pre-eminent in things Scottish and a sort of player in the higher British Establishment league. But that definition of 'Scottishness' was one that never required the need for political power, or for problem solving within our borders. Nor did it seek a view of the world, sentiment and shipping aside, that was founded on a viewpoint from anywhere but Westminster, the home of all good things democratic.

It was not always so. Muir remarks on the distinctive Scottish nature of Edinburgh, and the way in which it is founded on Knox and Melville and on the enlightenment. But while Scottishness was stirring elsewhere – while Tom Johnston, the greatest Secretary of State, was re-vitalising the rural North and Bob Grieve was struggling with the regeneration of Glasgow – Edinburgh seemed to turn even more towards the south and towards its faded glory as a partner in the British adventure. Certainly there were people who were swimming against that tide, but the overall impression was one of a determination not to give way to the forces that were slowly re-shaping our sense of identity. Edinburgh, it seemed to say to itself, was above all that and would be the bulwark on which Scotland as part of Britain would be saved.

So the Edinburgh Festival came into being, not as a celebration of Scotland's place in the international world of the arts, but as a type of self-denying ordinance of Scottishness

– an event that said that high culture was more important than any pitiful localised expression of self-worth, and one which accrued to itself the most gigantic Footlights folly in the world, complete with Oxbridge undergraduates and the annual excursion of the metropolitan arts glitterati on holiday to the North. Of course that view of 'Scottishness' was far from being unique in pre- or post-war Edinburgh. In the upper and upper-middle classes being Scottish was not much different from being a Mason – an attachment rather than a definition. The golf club houses Edinburgh – or at least the grander ones ('Honourable Company' and all that) are still some of the least Scottish places you can visit without leaving the country, with an air of aspiration towards the golden days of Sunningdale, Edward VIII and PG Wodehouse rather than the bracing links of Troon or St Andrews. Working-class Edinburgh was different but there the fulfilment of the Scottish dimension was done by placing faith in either religion (usually Catholicism, as Presbyterianism in Edinburgh is a matter of wealthy churches and social mobility) or socialism.

Both flourished in the Edinburgh slums – the Blessed Margaret Sinclair showing one example and a succession of trade unionists another – and both survive in the peripheral housing estates. These were not in existence when Muir wrote about Edinburgh, but they dominate the outskirts of the city today: Wester Hailes, Granton, Pilton, Craigmillar and Gilmerton.

I cut my political teeth canvassing for Labour in some of these estates, but I needn't have bothered. Those that voted, voted Labour and returned Labour councillor after Labour councillor. But Edinburgh, perhaps gerrymandered in some deep way, kept on returning Tory MPs and Tory councils. Edinburgh was the last city in Scotland to have a majority of Tory parliamentarians, a situation that only changed in the 1980s. The city council's seemingly impregnable Labour majority is a matter of only the recent past, with the combined Liberal, Tory and (tiny) SNP groups technically able to deny Labour the administration as recently as 1992.

And the city's periphery is gaining its own periphery – the new private housing estates built with profit in mind and devoid of distinction, with the occasional 'executive' developments amongst them, designed for conspicuous consumers of the 21st century in the way that my grandparents' solid house in Inverleith Place contained the same types in the early 20th. Astonished as he would have been at the desire of Scotland for change, I suspect my grandfather would have been even more astonished to discover one of his family taking part in the process. Politics and disputation I take from my father – the Russell side – not from the Haynes' – my mother's.

Swashing about with family thoughts that have not occurred to me for more than two decades, I walk up towards Tanfield, viewing with a cold eye the modern office development that has replaced the grim printing works, and walk back to the Botanic Gardens. The winter clientele consists of old ladies, dogs and some teenagers who are probably meant to be somewhere else. But the view (always the view in Edinburgh) is spectacular, with the castle rock dominating a landscape of steeples.

In a nearby café I get talking to one of the women, perhaps aged about 60, who is Edinburgh to her fingertips and who is taking shelter from the drizzle that has started again. 'Parliament...', she starts with ill-disguised contempt, '... parliament is in London – this will just be a lot of politicians with nothing to do – more cost and more interference.' She has voted NO NO at the referendum and cannot see why anyone should be discontented in Scotland: there are lots of jobs for those that want them, and houses too. She does not want to tell me to my face that nationalism is just troublemaking, but she gets the message across. Then she leaves for home with a frosty-faced smile cracking her features. If there is anyone waiting for her there, they must be dreading her return.

I have given myself a day in Edinburgh, but already it is turning dark and the afternoon is running on. I take a bus across the city, ending up at Pollock Halls of Residence, the main student accommodation for Edinburgh University, whose tiny windows are slowly lighting up as lectures finish and socialising or studying begins. I find a student pub and savour a drink, listening to the gossip around me. It is hard to start a conversation here that does not sound like a pick-up line but two English students next to me slowly open up and reveal a deep interest in what I am asking. They are studying politics and are keen to show their sympathy with what Scotland wants; though they (like me) are not sure what that is. In their second year they are excited by the Blairite revolution (they call it that) but are surprisingly sympathetic to Thatcher – the Tories deserved to lose because they didn't value her, it appears.

In the 70s Edinburgh University was the home of the far left, occupations, sit-ins and a student newspaper so radical that it refused to appoint a friend and me as editors because (being in the Labour party) we were too far to the right. Compared to the Blair revolution I was a Trotskyite though there were real Trotskyites then who were elected members of the Student Representative Council and who now pop up from time to time as respectable publishers, cautious broadcasters or even putative government ministers. Perhaps a bar at 5pm is not the place to seek them, but the radicals of today seem more timid than even before. I am glad that I am with Robert Frost on this: 'I dared not be radical when young, for fear I'd be conservative when old'.

The students are off to a late seminar but politely wish me well with the book and leave me with a parting thought – Scotland can choose what it wants and no-one will object. 'Only ourselves,' I think, as the clientele shifts towards an Edinburgh bias with office workers and the odd pair of overalls filling up the available spaces. The talk is all of football.

It is by now quite dark but I have two places I still want to visit. I walk across the city, along the Meadows with its wonderful expanse of grass and trees backing onto the university and make my way down towards Gorgie and Dalry. These were the peripheral estates of the late-19th century, steep tenement housing for the lower-middle and upper working classes and now a hotch potch of cheap shops, Chinese restaurants, restored first-time buyer's flats, students' shared apartments and homes for all ages who have enough capital for a foot on the house-owning ladder.

The narrow streets of the main thoroughfares are crowded with cars – two-deep already in some places. The pavements have rubbish sacks at the edge, for tomorrow's refuse collection (despite firm admonitions in all the closes about rubbish only being put out on the day of collection) and there is the inevitable dog shit every hundred yards or so (Edinburgh election meetings are dominated by the defecatory practices of dogs and how to control them. Any political party that offers canine colostomy is on to a winner).

There are streets like this all over the capital – in Stockbridge, in Newington, in Leith, even in up-market Blackhall – and in various degrees they represent the bulk of city life, though, along with the housing estates, they are the least visited. If the new parliament, still a wraith of an idea shimmering over Holyrood, is to mean anything to Edinburgh it must mean something to the people who live here. The first pub in which I intend to sample opinion has half a dozen mean-faced old men huddled round the bar, whose collective scowls on my entry make me gulp a drink and leave without conversation.

The second pub is warmer and more varied. Three drinks have had their effect and made me more gallus, so I start asking questions while I am still at the bar. Politics is not uppermost in their minds, but change is – change more radical and more domestic than that for which (they admit) they all voted Labour as recently as last May. Two or three see no point in talking about the parliament, but John – fiftyish, working in a small engineering company – admits to being interested and hopeful. 'The way I see it, ken, is that we need our own folk in there and we need to start daein' somethin' fir oorsels, ken.' He worries, he says, about his own job and about his weans – one of whom is looking for a job. 'I want him here', he says, 'or at least wi' the choice o' being here'.

John is Edinburgh born and bred. He has never heard of Edwin Muir but he loves the city. He mentions with pride the bits of its history he knows, and refers to Sean Connery as its greatest son. When I tell him that I have met Connery, my stock rises though it drops again when a wee old guy says he was at school with him, a story they have all heard before. It is the type of bar where I could happily sit all evening, but I have one last call to make. I stand at the bus stop waiting to return to Princes Street, and there is one other person by the shelter. He has a livid birthmark on his face – the type that it is hard not to look at – and a roving eye, with the Ancient Mariner look in it. I am not going to talk, but he is – first of all about the time it takes to wait for a bus, then about the weather, then about the young people passing by. Monosyllables in reply don't staunch the flow: longer answers only encourage him. We are soon on to betting (I don't, neither does he), drinking (he doesn't), smoking (I am, he thinks it's a waste of money) and still the bloody bus doesn't come.

A woman joins the queue but the conversationalist still has me in his sights. I am beginning to feel desperate, the more so as he is also going to Princes Street. I stop answering, just nodding mutely, and this slows him down. He eyes the women as a possible talking partner, but sensibly she is minutely studying her shoes. Still the bus doesn't come.

He has now started to ask me what I do and where I come from. An ideal opportunity to ask him about his parliament but I dread the cascade of opinions that this is bound to unleash. Another person joins the queue, and he looks hopefully at them. I am ready now to grab any bus, anywhere (risking his censure as he realises I am about to be carried to the wrong place) when round the corner comes the Number 3. He gets on first and I watch where he is going. I then place myself as far away as possible, but his affections are fickle – I am no sooner seated than I can hear him starting all over again with the poor girl he is squashing into the window as he leans towards her.

I alight again at the foot of Lothian Road, but this time turn into the New Town and towards Charlotte Square. The rain has stopped and the clouds are clearing – its getting cold, the very best time to walk through James Craig's masterpiece of Georgian planning. Even when I was at university I used to come to this part of town on a winter evening to walk along George Street and down to Heriot Row. The streets – almost empty even at this early hour – ring to the footsteps and where there are still houses occupied there are glimpses of well hung sashes, antique furniture, pools of light from table lamps and the shadows of people within.

Georgian Edinburgh was the site of the greatest spectacles of the 'King's Jaunt' – the return of a monarch to Edinburgh in 1822 after a century and a half of absence. Scott not only invented tartanry to dress it – the begetter of a multi-million pound industry and the abiding image of Scotland – he also uncovered the Scottish Crown Jewels and stage-managed the creation of a country that still lives in fiction.

But Georgian Edinburgh was much more than a backdrop for royalty. It was the embodiment of the triumph of ideas and the solidification of the enlightenment into an expression of how people should live and view the world. They do, as Muir said, show how to live a 'rational city life', even though that life was available only to the very few. I walk past Scott's house in Castle Street, where he wrote, first of all to entertain and express his creative abilities, and then to pay off the mountain of debt that towered over him and which oppressed his every waking moment. Payment by the yard was what he sought, and yet he could still express something of the spirit of his country in novels such as *Old Mortality* and in occasionally sparkling verse. He entertained Robert Burns – that other voice of the land – and was the mouthpiece for an accepted view of his country that still saw less good in the Union than later historians would have us believe. The view, that he puts into his *Letters of Malachi Malagrowther* that says:

> For God's sake, sir, let us remain as Nature made us,
> Englishmen, Irishmen and Scotchmen with something like the
> impress of our several countries upon each.

And goes on to claim that:

> *The degree of national diversity between different countries is but an instance of that general variety which Nature seems to have adopted as a principle through all her works, as anxious, apparently, to avoid, as modern statesmen to enforce, anything like an approach to absolute uniformity.*

It is the New Town of Edinburgh that expresses – for me – almost better than anything else in Edinburgh, the national diversity that sets apart Scotland from other countries. The Castle is grand, and the Old Town entertaining and full of personality. The outlying areas are in varying degrees pleasant, depressing, blighted or plain ordinary. But the New Town is unique – despite all the depredations and its strangulation by offices that, until recently, filled more and more of its magnificent buildings. It is the New Town that speaks of a desire to improve, to change, to progress and which has taken those aspirations to solid perfection and which speaks also of how those things can be achieved in Scotland and how the best can be made here. The spirit that made the New Town – the 'boldness of foresight and standard of achievement' according to Muir – is a spirit that can make a new parliament. And not just a fine parliament building, but also a fine institution, at work for the people it is made to serve.

Perhaps not everyone is as excited by that prospect as I am. Or perhaps the Edinburgh reserve or cynicism doesn't let them express it. Now it is time to find out if outside the city walls there is more openness about the matter, and new perspectives that are not blunted by the Edinburgh winds and the psychological factors which distance Edinburgh from the rest of Scotland.

I turn up my coat collar and head for my car. Time to go south and west.

Chapter Three
The Borders, Dumfries and Galloway

'I left Edinburgh on a bright July Sunday in a 1921 Standard car', writes Muir, in a good mood for a change, as he gets his journey underway. I didn't. I was in a three-year-old Land-Rover Discovery, and although therefore more comfortable, there was the downside of it being neither bright, nor July – just winter, rainy with a gusting wind that would make any excursion to look at the landscape a matter of careful consideration. I was also vaguely uneasy, because I was about to depart from Muir's footsteps. He had gone south to the Border towns, intending to spend the night in Jedburgh and take what he called 'an easy run' to Galashiels, Melrose and Dryburgh.

Much of my consideration about what to see and write about in Scotland had been formed by what I already knew – places and people where I could apply some yardstick of how this country was changing and where it wanted to go. Keen as I was to use Muir as the baseline for the journey, it seemed foolish to see places for the first time through his eyes. And although I had been to Jedburgh (once) and had stayed in Galashiels for several nights in early 1974, campaigning for David Graham as 'Labour's Young man for the Borders' – though on election day in February I went back to Edinburgh and voted SNP for the first time – I hardly know the Border country and its curious mixture of mills, ruined monasteries and sweeties: Jeddart Snails, Hawick Balls and Moffat Toffee.

One of the odd things about Scotland is the ill-travelled nature of most of its inhabitants. That is not to say that they don't get about – vast crowds throng the airports and the motorways south during the traditional holiday times of the Glasgow Fair and the Edinburgh Trades. Thousands travel backwards and forwards from one city to another every day, driving lorries, selling mobile phones and doing all the things that our ancestors didn't do. But having detailed knowledge of more than one or two parts of this comparatively small country is rare. In 40 odd years I have lived in Fife, Ayrshire, the Western Isles, by Loch Ness, Edinburgh, Lanarkshire and I currently reside in Argyll. That makes me almost a professional gypsy compared to most of my friends, who may have moved from their home town to university and then on to their present location but have done little more.

Perhaps one of the vestiges of dependency is a lack of curiosity about one's own country. If the TV makes Scots viewers more familiar with Brookside Close and Downing Street than with Wick and Wigtown, then it is scarcely surprising that travel ambitions are fulfilled by getting out of Scotland rather than travelling through it. And living in a country that doesn't specialise in sunshine is a factor not to be forgotten. As if trying to make sure I don't forget it, the rain turns torrential. The Land-Rover seems to be sailing, not driving, through an endless wash and the flashing speed warning sign at West Linton won't be needed to remind me to be sensible. I am in no hurry anyway and as I can see little of the landscape through the downpour, I slow down to examine Edinburgh's hinterland and the edge of the Borders.

To the right of the road I am taking (that will bring me to the M74 at Abington and the main route south towards England) are the Pentland Hills, in which the Battle of Rullion Green took place in 1666. Its bloody and inevitable outcome was the final defeat of the Pentlands' Rising, which had previously re-affirmed at Lanark the 'glorious marriage of the Kingdom of God'. Those in defence of that Scottish faith and that Scottish view of the contract between God and his people, had then moved to the gates of Edinburgh. But the city did not rise to help and after a dispirited withdrawal via Colinton, the army of the Covenant was surrounded in atrocious weather (November but like today really) on the slopes of Carnethy. There they resisted for as long as possible the trained troops led by Sir Tam Dalyell, Black Tam of the Binns. With 50 dead and 80 taken prisoner the Lord did not save them or their cause, and the lucky ones ended up in Barbados. The unlucky ones – 36 of them – were hanged.

The Covenant is one of those recurring episodes in Scottish History in which the force of an idea becomes stronger than good sense and drives on more and more people to suffering and death. The 'Lords of the Covenant' first subscribed to the notion of a peculiar (in the best sense) Scottish bond between God and the people prior to the Reformation, and re- affirmed it regularly thereafter. The National Covenant of 1638 became a public petition, presuming a direct Scottish relationship with God (excluding from that relationship not just 'Papistry' but also the King) and, in citing over 60 Acts of the Scottish Parliament, made a declaration of rights that attracted 300,000 signatures, attested at churches throughout the land.

Cromwellian duplicity prevented the later 'Solemn League and Covenant' (Scots have always been good at grand titles) from taking effect as the underpinning governance of Scotland but Cromwell misjudged Scottish opinion by assuming that regicide could be compassed by covenanting principles. It could not, and his occupation of Scotland was required to prevent further war. Charles II had to sign the Covenant to get Scottish support for his coronation at Scone in 1651, before fleeing abroad. He quickly disowned it at the Restoration and instead enforced a religious policy that favoured Episcopalianism. Back came the resistance and the classic conventicles, where armed guards protected outdoor Presbyterian worship.

The defeat of one Covenanters' rising was usually followed by the start of another. Rullion Green gave way to Drumclog, a bleak bit of ground between Kilmarnock and Strathaven (whose fields still possess the air of a battleground and the feeling of endless forgotten bodies underfoot) and Bothwell Brig, in Lanarkshire. And as in most passionate Scottish beliefs, success was not victory enough. The Presbyterian settlement of 1690 did not satisfy the extremists and the Covenant and its principles threaded on through Scottish church history, though they were increasingly inaccurately invoked. To me, as an Episcopalian, it seems as if the Covenanters won, and Episcopalianism was tarnished forever by its association with oppression and persecution. The Killing Times far outweigh in most Scots' minds the murder of the Episcopalian Archbishop Sharp at the sinisterly named Magus Moor near St Andrews.

Today, glancing at the hills as I drive along, they seem irrevocably in mourning for those who huddled in their linns and corries as the government soldiers drove down. About a decade ago the same hills witnessed another murder in uniform when a serving soldier from the nearby barracks gunned down his colleagues to get hold of the army payroll. Those murders did not go unpunished, but have ever since stuck in my mind as being almost literary in their plotting and execution.

I am getting gloomy, and the little villages I pass through do not raise my mood. They are not much more than lines of cottages beside the road, and the sight of larger houses away up side roads remind me that I am still within commuting distance of Edinburgh. But soon I am past the flashing speed sign and out of West Linton, which, since an earlier visit that confirmed my suspicion that it is a village too quiet by far, I have decided not to detour into.

Between here and Biggar there is not much to see or think about. Signposts indicate roads from time to time which lead to places I know – Peebles with its grand Hydro, Johannesburg Bridge over the Tweed and its wide main street and Lanark where my son was born and which I will try and visit when I return north. A few miles further on and the countryside changes again, becoming more wooded – more Borders like – until I sweep into the broad expanse of Biggar's main street, in the middle of which every Hogmanay there have a huge communal bonfire to welcome in the New Year. It never fails to make a picture for the Scottish press the next day and generates tiresome letters about tradition versus safety for three further editions.

Biggar is Scotland's museum town – it has what one commentator called 'museum mania', an affliction that is striking more and more of Scotland. Not only can you visit Gladstone Court, a 'street museum' complete with shops (the name reminding the curious that Biggar was the home of William Ewart Gladstone's forebears), but you can also see, as a 'museumed' piece, the site where Wallace is said to have defeated a much larger English army in 1287. Then you can toddle off to a ('museumed') Covenanter's Farm House, leaf through the archives of the ('museumed') Albion Motor Company – one of Scotland's first car manufacturers – and then, on a downhill spiral of interest, end up at the ('museumed') Biggar Gas works. This is probably the most boring museum in the world, unless there is one made out of a disused sewage farm somewhere, illustrating by means of display boards the processing of shit. On a scale of interest from one to ten, the museum made out of Biggar Gas works rates less than zero. I suspect that those who worked there in the 19th century found it interminably boring and thus the mindset of its keepers in the Royal Scottish Museum who regard it as an underdeveloped tourist attraction is a matter of amazement. It might just about enthral one of those strange PhD students, burrowing in the specialist subject of 'Domestic Fuel Production Technology in late-Victorian Scotland' but for anyone else – and let me advise you most strongly – it would be far more profitable to repair to one of the town's little tea shops or enjoy a wonderful ice cream in the Townhead Café. It would be even be more enjoyable to just carry on standing in the rain waiting to be ground down in geological time by erosion.

On the road from Biggar to the M74 are a couple of villages, Coulter being the largest, which are centred around large houses – the remnants of landed estates which for the most part have fragmented. In Coulter the 'big house' is owned by Arthur Bell, a political activist who runs a mail order company and who has recently forsaken a Scottish Tory party that never listened to him for a Liberal Party that may not want to. As the jobs for the people for whom these houses were built have disappeared, so has the cohesion of the villages themselves – they look loosened-off, and perhaps appear to hang apart somewhat. It is a strange impression, probably brought about by the diversity of door and window colours, different types of curtains and different uses for gardens. It is, in a genteel sort of way, the same type of effect that is obvious in larger villages full of council houses that still exist in Ayrshire and Lanarkshire. Erected for those who worked in the local pits, the removal of the unifying purpose has spun the centre out of the community. Economically it may have survived, even prospered as people buy their houses and as commuters move in. But it is not hard to tell that the shared experience has gone (perhaps, given its grind and – in the feudal villages at least – its lack of dignity, that is no bad thing).

After negotiating the new and very confusing junction which also serves the old A74, I slip onto the M74. The conversion to motorway status is about the only lasting monument to the last 18 years of Tory rule in Scotland. For years the A74 was regarded as a death trap. Dual carriageway in the main, its traffic had an overload of heavy lorries which thundered past the more sedate domestic traffic, only to grind to a halt behind the inevitable farm tractor and trailer, or the local school bus between stops. Eventually the Scottish Office capitulated after the Tories offered upgrading in order to secure votes a couple of General Elections ago. The Tories won and so the work began. It is still not finished.

Upgrading the road was sensible – but it produced an atavistic response from the father of one of my son's school friends, himself a lorry driver – who rang me to ask if I would help him organise a petition and a campaign to stop the renaming of the motorway. Planners, being logical souls, have decreed that it should, on completion, become the M6, as it is (it cannot be denied) a linear extension of that motorway which starts at Spaghetti Junction in Birmingham. This type of response to even sensible, non-controversial details of change is mirrored in letters I get every week from Scots – often not nationalists – who react with horror at supposed slights on their country. Some are even less substantial than this – the design of breakfast cereal packets, or an advertisement for beer. Certainly many of these changes are thoughtless and unduly centralising and individuals may usefully prick the bubble of complacency and ignorance that gives rise to them. But were a political party to base its actions and its case on candy floss, it would serve the cause of change no service at all. Once this attitude has a grip, the party loses its grander, more vital, vision.

Personally I couldn't care less what the road is called as long as Scotland gets better transport links for its industries and better communications with our neighbours in the south. But if the Government believes that by incorporating a road designation more firmly into a British scheme they are tying the bonds of Union every more tightly, then they are already on the road to failure – obsessed with symbols and not substance. My lorry-driving friend didn't see it that way – he and his colleagues viewed the name change as a threat to their sense of national identity and wanted the SNP to intervene.

We didn't. We might have in the past, and maybe we still do sometimes in some seemingly silly matters, but at a time when the process of change is so firmly underway, stopping to protest at the trivial means there is less time for the essential. This syndrome was apparent during the ill-fated Garscadden by-election in 1977 when a daft argument was raging within the SNP about 'designing the epaulettes on the uniforms for a proposed Scottish army'. While it inflamed the party's internal passions it was utterly meaningless to the millions of voters who hadn't yet decided whether Scotland should even have a parliament. Our new parliament should be sensible enough to share a system of road classification with England, or better still with Europe, although it will always be the M74 to me no matter what its new designation will be.

Muir came to this artery of UK communication from the east, crossing from the Borders to Moffat and then might have taken to the meandering road that worked its way south past the hamlets of Wamphray and Dinwoodie Green and on through the town of Lockerbie, ancestral home to one of the families involved in the vast Hong Kong trading company of Jardine-Matheson. Further south is the village of Ecclefechan, birthplace of Thomas Carlyle, who was thus handily situated to get out of Scotland to live the life of a supposedly authentic Scottish sage well furth of its Borders, (had he been closer to home his pretensions might have been harder to get away with) and Gretna – the marriage capital of Europe, according to the tourist hyperbole. Muir's other option was simply to continue from Moffat towards Dumfries and on the basis that he did, I follow suit.

He found this countryside full of 'signs of fruitfulness' and decided that here 'fertility is a solid organised industry'. Certainly compared to the sparseness of the hill country to the north we are now coming back down into the more favoured plains. The proliferation of side roads – farm roads, little tarmacadamed winding lanes to villages, country drives to large houses, many of which now seem to be nursing homes or religious or New Age retreats – increases and trees have an ordered, domesticated but rather ancient look. But they are broadleaves, not the regimented rows of Sitka spruce plantations on the higher hill ground. This part of Dumfriesshire, north of Lochmaben and surrounding Parkgate and Amisfield is countryside that still has agriculture as its major industry and still sustains dairy farming which has been driven out by (paradoxically) deregulation in so many other areas. Heavily-laden cows occasionally trudge across the landscape on their way to be relieved of their painful, liquid burdens. Further on, past Dumfries there is even a special set of traffic lights for one farm that allows its herd to cross the main road twice a day.

But this bucolic idyll disguises the truth of farming today in Dumfriesshire, or anywhere else in Scotland. Farm suicides are at their highest ever level: banks are talking about the unthinkable, foreclosing on agricultural lending. Muir's 'rich agricultural county' and his mind 'insensibly filled with thoughts of livestock, cattle-shows, prize bulls and Scots love in the Burns style' speaks of another age, Georgian in its plenty. And healthy in its closeness to the soil, challenged as we are with BSE, E. coli, salmonella and all the other scares that do as much damage to our confidence in life as they do to our constitutions.

But there is still a suspicious look of prosperity to these farms as I pass, and I think of the suspicions that most people harbour about farmers: that they cry ' wolf', expecting the state to support them and all that sort of thing. Surely if farm incomes were collapsing we would start to see broken fences, unmended roofs, fields full of weeds and tares and emaciated cattle stumbling about. There is none of that here – and there is still the glint of the bonnet of a new Volvo estate as the fleeting sun peers into a farmyard and the rumbling roar of a new tractor bullying its way down a narrow lane.

Anyone who lives in a rural community, as I do, knows the pub stories about farmers. So and so has an overdraft of £100,000 but buys a new car every year; someone else comes in in his wellie boots stinking of shit, but his wife is off to a health farm for a fortnight. The very success of farmers in establishing an unrivalled system of state support and a lobbying machine of the greatest power has created resentment. There is a feeling that farmers have profited too much from the taxpayer and that a little bit of hardship might not be too bad a thing to teach them a lesson.

But we need farming more than ever. Not just because we

need food, and a secure domestic supply of essentials: more and more we can import though that is a route to shortage and hardship if times change. But we also need something to underpin the rural economy when schools are closing, shops are shutting and transport is rapidly becoming non-existent. Certainly today there are not three 'orra men' and a boy on every steading, but there is a continuity of family employment and a reason for at least one son (or daughter) of the family to stay at home and carry on with something built for him or her and which he or she can build for a future generation. My neighbour in Argyll, Archie McNaughton, talks of a time when farming was 'all there was in the Glen' and speaks of it as a better time when there were children going to the now nearly empty school and a viable shop in the community. It is not just the decline of farming that has changed that, but it has been one of the factors. I shall return, I am sure, to this problem that confronts anyone who travels in rural Scotland today, but already I am on the outskirts of Dumfries having passed the sign for the village with the shortest place name in Scotland – Ae. (Not the shortest name, though. That honour belongs to the Gaelic name for Iona, the splendid single *I*).

Dumfries, like all Scottish county towns, has grown out of its natural boundaries, and spreads now like a dowager at every extremity. And just as the borders have bulged and given way to a variety of largely ugly housing estates, the heart has been eaten up by new shop fronts – though at least here they still sit in mostly older buildings and one can still sense something of the town as it was well before Muir, who, even 60 years ago, called it a 'blowsy, overgrown country town' and who thought it of interest only because Maxwelltown, of Annie Laurie fame, was now within its boundaries. Muir may have been mistaken – the association is more likely with Maxwelton House, a few miles further north up the Cairn Valley.

Dumfries deserves more than a casual glance, however. I find a parking space on the Whitesands – still a lovely riverside spot despite the acres of tarmac dominated by the car. The River Nith in Dumfries is unlike most rivers in Scottish towns because it gives the impression not of gentle descent but of untrammelled power – and it bursts its banks on regular occasions, requiring radio alerts to careless commuters whose vehicles are about to sink beneath the waves. I don't think I have ever been in Dumfries without seeing a sandbag, kept in readiness for the regular inundations. The town centre – with its back to the river – has the usual sprinkling of chain stores and the usual complement of skinny, ill-dressed women in their early twenties who seem to hover around cheap Scottish shops like importuning wraiths. These are the marginal people of Scottish society, existing on poorly paid part-time jobs or inadequate benefits, living from night out to night out. They are as much victims of poor living conditions as the unemployed that Muir saw hanging about on street corners 60 years ago.

I talk to two of them at the mouth of the Vennel – the alleyway that leads up to Burns Square. Both are unemployed, both are single mothers, and both are curious that there might be some ulterior motive for me seeking them out – perhaps a Social Security enquiry. They have remarkably little sense of grievance against the society that has done precious little for them – the poverty of their ambition is irking. They want not much more than a decent house (and they are doing their best to make their own council homes into that desirable state), clothes and toys for the 'kiddies', and the money to have a drink and a laugh with friends. One – Jeanette – has never voted and doesn't think it's worth the effort. The other – Susan – has voted Labour all her life but 'disnae see anything changing.' She might vote SNP, more likely than not as she thinks about it, because she knows her benefit is under threat.

They are both unsure about what the new parliament will do for them. Perhaps give them more money, perhaps pay some attention to child care. Perhaps even help them get a job. And they have no ideas at all about what they want from the parliament. The question hangs in the air and they seem disinterested in answering it. There are thousands of Jeanettes and Susans the length and breadth of Scotland who are perhaps not in the direst poverty, but for whom there is little chance of a better life short of winning the national lottery. And thousands for whom politics is not even of casual interest and for whom a new parliament has a vague association with Scottishness and themselves, but no association with anything that they might actually aspire to.

But there are also thousands of Sallys. Working in an upmarket chain store she is ambitious, about to get married and political in the sense that she votes and tries to think about what choice would be best for her future. She has voted Tory in the past – some people still do – and might again, but they aren't Scottish enough for her and she giggles at the thought of William Hague in a kilt. She wants prosperity, peace, jobs, and although the government won't and shouldn't do it all, at least it should help. Her boyfriend arrives when I am talking to her and takes a dim view of what he thinks is a chat up. Reassured by her he still looks sideways at me as she serves and talks at the same time, to the annoyance of her customers.

Thousands of Sallys to counterpoint thousands of Susans. The world split between those who want something and are out to get it, and those who started with a losing hand and can see no point in not going on playing it. The wannabes meet the have-nots for the great gameshow of our time, and politicians know little if anything about it.

We are now firmly in Burns country. He would doubtless have been attracted to Sally with the little butterfly tattooed on her ankle, but pitifully sorrowful for Susan and Jeanette. And in Burns country all the signs point to places where the bard stopped, or drank in, or tilled the soil until exhaustion and heartbreak carried him away. Unlike, however, the endless sites associated with Mary Queen of Scots most of the Burns' ones are genuine and often touching. In Dumfries one can drink in the snug bar at the Globe Inn where Burns drank with his cronies and experience the small, cramped surroundings. Here Burns took the King's shilling as an excise man – proving again, if proof was needed, that consistency in poets is not to be looked for.

Despite the modern office buildings and the trendy road signs, Dumfries always strikes me as a town with more honest history and roots than many others in Scotland. Perhaps it is because the whole of Galloway is comparatively unvisited and more solidly Scottish than those places which have recast their face for tourists. Or perhaps because as a child I remember being driven through it on the way to our annual holidays either south of the Border or in Ireland. It seems to have changed so little – even the Station Hotel, where we took lunch each time – is just the same.

Or perhaps not. Certainly it is old-fashioned and the food as plastic as you get without actually chewing on Tupperware, but there are plush seats that are clearly the product of a 1990's interior designer, trapped in a time warp and forced to work 20 years behind the times. There are leaflets at reception advertising health clubs and a range of tourist attractions each more gaudy than the last. I eat a solitary lunch and look at the station yard – Dumfries is lucky enough still to have a station, although trains are both rare and rarely on time. Privatisation may have produced a rash of new rail logos but the old photographs of Dumfries station wreathed in good old fashioned steam-engine smoke make the place look much more efficient and much more devoted to getting the traveller from A to B in the most effective and timeous fashion.

The rain has petered out now, but at two in the afternoon evening is not far away in a Scottish winter. I make my way back to the Discovery and head over Buccleuch Street Bridge to take the road towards Kirkcudbright, not just because Muir did so (on a gloriously hot day, of course) but because it is a road that I know well. I have travelled it every six weeks or so since the early 1970s when my parents moved to the douce little town that they had previously never even visited.

As the road unwinds the sense of history stays with me. Ninemile Bar (Crocketford) is just a crossroads with a wee hotel and some terraced houses but it must have grown up with a purpose – a way station for the unimaginably long distances between towns and villages which our century has shrunk to nearly nothing. Springholm – for years a single street with houses mostly on one side along with a shop and the wonderfully named 'Reoch Hotel' – has gained a new housing estate, a 'Brookside of the North' for would-be executives to come home to. What are they executives *of* in Springholm, I wonder...

I ignore the Castle Douglas by-pass and drive down the long straight main street, bustling with traffic and shoppers. The name of the town itself is redolent with history, and there is a good country feel to the place – farmers in to collect some sheep dip, or a part for the tractor, the district nurse catching up on her messages in between calls. We are all sentimental for the supposed good old days, the days of simplicity and crises packaged for Dr Finlay's Casebook. That is a Scotland we regard with affection, aware of course that it never really existed and is part of the kailyard legacy.

Ten minutes later I am in Kirkcudbright, where Muir met up with the 'vanguard of the long procession of English tourists who kept up with me during all my road to the north of Scotland'. Cosmopolitan Muir was offended by the sense of isolation that they possessed, their 'exasperating habit of filling a foreign country with the local atmosphere of some provincial or suburban district of their own land'.

He goes on: 'When they appear in a foreign hotel or public room it is as if they were preceded by an invisible vacuum cleaner which removes all trace of local associations so that they may comfortably settle in with the customary aura of their existence quite complete and inviolate around them like a vast immaterial cushion. So I found Maidenhead in Dunkeld, Brixton in Ullapool and Tunbridge Wells in Scourie.'

No one who has travelled in Scotland can fail to recognise what Muir was saying. The same condition can be witnessed today in any of the favourite English package holiday destinations abroad. You can come off a yacht in the smallest of Greek harbours, and be taken aback by the glimpse of a painted Union Jack on a taverna wall, with the legend 'English breakfasts, English Pub, English Landlord'. And if you are foolish enough to seek it out, that is exactly what it offers – a bit of England on a foreign field or quayside, with the English happily ensconced *contra mundum.*

Yet it was as difficult for a Scottish writer to comment on the English in Muir's time as it is in ours. He hedges his comments about them with compliments ('I have a great admiration for the English people, who are a most civilised race') in the hope of softening the blow of his criticism. We are conditioned to avoid speaking in public about the matter, for fear that anything we do say will be taken down and used against us – evidence of racism or chauvinism. And for me there is an added complication. I was born in England, and my mother (though raised in Scotland) was happy until recently to call herself English (although after living here for around 70 years, being married here, having children and eventually voting SNP seem to have brought her to a more reasonable definition of herself – Scottish now, she says, but of an English father!).

Little matter that I lived in the land of my birth for less than nine months (and all of those as an infant), I still find it difficult to criticise the English too closely. And yet the whole question of the English in Scotland – living, visiting or ruling – is one that needs to be discussed if we are to set aside the prejudices that have surrounded the subject for years. There is undoubtedly knee-jerk anti-Englishness in Scotland, but it exists at a low level and is no more destructive or prone to action than the knee-jerk anti-Edinburgh sentiments you can stir up in a Glasgow pub with a single remark, and a good deal less harmful than the anti-Gaelic feelings that still run through some of Lowland Scotland. It says as much about Scottish insecurity as anything else. They are, of course, in many ways a good, decent and noble people – I am far from ashamed of where my maternal grandfather came from and far from ashamed of his yeoman ancestors.

There have been attempts in recent years to elevate this atavistic activity into some form of major racism and to use it to assert that there is a 'problem' with Scotland and in particular with Nationalism. Certainly Scotland would be better off without it, but go to France and ask about Germany (indeed go to England and ask about Germany) and the response will be far more virulent and far more likely to result in real acts of discrimination or hostility. The ridiculous scenes the world witnessed as English football 'fans' rampaged through French and Belgian towns and ports during this summer's World Cup cast a much longer and darker shadow than anything in Scotland today – and contrasted dramatically with the open-handed internationalism of the Tartan Army.

In fact the surprising thing in Scotland is the way in which anti-Englishness has not become part of the political scene. There is no doubt that what Muir observed is an irritant to Scots, but there are many English people living in and visiting Scotland who participate and adapt in the way that Scots throughout the world do: retaining a level of cultural affinity with their country of origin while taking part fully in community life and sharing community aspirations and goals. There are some others, however, who seek to turn Tighnabruaich into Tunbridge Wells and who elbow out the diffident or the taciturn Scots and dominate every local committee and every local decision. And not just dominate but turn the focus into a 'British' matter (for British read English) and drone on at dinner parties about Haywards Heath and Hampstead as if they were round the corner, not 400 miles down the road, and as if everyone shared their knowledge of, and affection for, and family links with, such places.

The bus parties that crowd into the paper shop in Arrochar where I buy my *Herald* on the way to Edinburgh carry with them their towns and cities – and the detail of the life of those towns and cities – like turtles carrying their homes upon their backs. A few want the *Mirror* and the *Sun* and can't understand why they get something with the same name, but with 'Scottish' in front of it. These same regard being abroad (and they are abroad – culturally, socially and geographically) as being a state possible to ignore if they talk loud enough in public and they even resent the fact that Arrochar *is* abroad – it should be morphed into Watford or Woking as quickly as possible, with lochs and hills and preferably without the prickly natives.

It would be better for all of us if the natives weren't so prickly, if we learned (and we should have learned after all these years) that what is being expressed is just their way of seeing the world. That view is grounded in generations of insularity and a unique ability to pretend to internationalism while being fiercely, narrowly, national. We have had them as peaceful neighbours for generations and we should by now have got used to their foibles and affectations, just as we would like them to get used to our own. Margo MacDonald put it well when she looked forward to the day when England could win the World Cup and Scots say 'So what'. But that day will only come when we have the confidence to see ourselves as equals, and when that view is reciprocated. Until then there will always be a slight edge to the relationship and we will always find things that annoy us about some of the people who share this island.

But better to be annoyed than to be angry. And it is not an angry relationship.

Kirkcudbright has its share of English visitors – and also its share of English residents. Yet it still conveys that Galloway sense of history, perhaps even more than Dumfries. Although it too has sprawled out, with fringes covered in modern bungalows, its heart is not just well preserved but well lived in. Its houses have an austerity that sits well under the usually grey Solway sky (though they are still painted in a range of colours, which surprised Muir and which is uncommon in Scotland, Tobermory aside) and the wide streets are straight and straightforward.

Kirkcudbright is also an artists' town, its plain but stylish Scottishness and its surrounding hills appealing to Charles Rennie MacIntosh, Oppenheimer and to Hornel. The last-mentioned bequeathed his house to the town, along with a selection of paintings that are bright, romantic and direct. A community that can look after these but can also hold

'Scottish nights' in its riverside square complete with bagpipes for the tourists is a town at ease with itself; a town that can take on a new democracy and a new parliament and still get something out of it – and perhaps keep the best of itself, renewed again and again.

I arrive in Kirkcudbright in the dusk, the wet pavements sparkling in the glare of the streetlights. I negotiate the corner by the Masonic Arms and park outside my mother's small house in the historic 'Tanpits Lane', a name that conjures up past industry and more kailyard memories. I have been on and off the road for eight hours and passed through generations of Scottish history. But I always sleep well in Kirkcudbright, comforted in the small hours by the parish church clock, tolling the night away.

That sound is another Scottish symbol, rarer now than ever. I treasure it every time I hear it, which just shows how trapped (and comforted) I am too by the kailyard fantasy.

Chapter Four
The Ayrshire Coast

I have come to Kirkcudbright not just to visit, but also to speak at an SNP branch meeting. It is held in one of the town's hotels, which – as in all small Scottish tourist venues – has been tarted up, but which still carries the ghost of the down-at-heel air of 1960's Scottish stopping places. It must be in the air, or in the scent of the furniture polish they use. It is as if we are in a hologram, a virtual reality, pastel-coloured print simulation of what hotels are meant to be like today, and that when it is switched off we will be back with the sagging sofas, the cream paint and sticky carpets, smelling of cigarette smoke.

The party is going through an in-between time early in 1998. The good showings in the polls and the hectic excitement lie unknown ahead – behind us is the grind of the election and the September 97 referendum and some indications from the most recent parliamentary and local by-elections that our stock is on the rise. The meeting holds a sense of anticipation, but a lack of direction too.

There is room for a good psychological study of the type of people who join political parties and faithfully attend meetings. For myself I recognise in it the symptom of a need to belong. It was the same complex, I am sure, that led me to go from a childhood that included church three times a week to train as an Episcopal priest. It was a need to be a part of something, and to take (for it is me I am talking about) an active part – to shape and mould and influence and try and change things. Perhaps (it is still me) it is a need to be recognised and valued and to develop relationships based on shared goals and trust. Despite the inevitable boredom of meeting after meeting, year after year, I still get a buzz from a branch event such as this – and try to communicate it in what I say. We are all in this together, and there is much to aim for and attempt to achieve.

Political parties have failings like any human structure. There are tensions, disagreements, and elements of factionalism. But they are kept in check if a party at heart contains a common belief, and a common ambition. They may even, like base metals turning to gold, be put to good purpose. Tonight there are difficult questions, some soul-searching by individuals who need reassurance that we are doing the right thing in being positive and supportive about a parliament that still falls short of what we want. But the common aim is to achieve – to achieve the best for Scotland and for the people who live in it. If we have to go about that task in a more measured, more responsive way than we once thought we should – if we have to build more slowly and persuade more lengthily (and by example) that there is an overwhelming acceptance that we should do so. Perhaps the lesson the SNP has learned more profoundly than any other over the past year is the lesson of humility and consensus: the lesson that we are not just there to challenge people with the problem, and hector them when they do not see our solution. We are there to be part of the solution, working towards it as a party of Scotland, and for Scotland – not the party above Scotland, the clever dicks who snipe from the sidelines, never dirtying their hands by putting them to the heavy plough.

The meeting finishes with the inevitable cup of tea beside a home-baking stall, groaning with plenty. Funds are raised. In ones or twos people drift to the bar to continue the conversations and to widen them out so that high politics blends into the concerns of everyday life. We are down from the mountain, and have learnt the lesson of the Transfiguration: those things forever kept apart, for ever spoken of only in the holy of holies are those things that have little influence on the lives we have to lead.

Later on I join the branch convener for a drink in the pub round the corner from my mother's house. He has with him a pile of old minute books and leaflets – responding to my plea months ago that we should as a party take better care of our history. I have filled my office walls with memorabilia of the SNP: now he wants me to be the custodian of the minutiae – the decaying accounts of pound, shilling and pence balances from election campaigns, or raging rows, recorded in a cramped hand, about divisive issues now completely forgotten.

Part crippled by arthritis, he is still almost aglow with the excitement of the SNP win in Galloway at the last election. But slowly we move on to other things and the ways in which he can build his membership and gain the resources he will need to fight another election so soon. And not just one, but several because 1999 will contain local council polls and the European contest. Slowly we are back to the present-day reality that mirrors the contents of these red bound books that still lie on the table: the struggle to make things happen within the envelope of constraint and ordinary life – within the constraint of being human. We are sharing ideas and experiences – two very different people with very different backgrounds are belonging to something bigger than they are, and are trying to shape and help it.

The next morning I am journeying again: out of a Kirkcudbright that is cold and bright and driving by the back roads to Ayr and towards the town where I grew up.

I first drove this road in the opposite direction, in 1974 when my father surprised us all (at the age of 54) by deciding to finish his career somewhere different from the town he had grown up in, and returned to (at the age of 39) after the war,

Reuters, the consular corps and a spell as a small town grocer and wine merchant in Fife. He returned to university, finished the degree he had abandoned when he volunteered for the Argyll and Sutherland Highlanders after his first year, and started to teach in Irvine. But – in a way that I recognise because I have inherited it – he was always dissatisfied and resolved to change yet again, looking for a place that was more in keeping with his idea of what life should be like. So he found Kirkcudbright, and he and my mother moved there – he to take up a post at the academy, she to look after an empty house, as her three sons were all away from home by then.

He should have known that it wouldn't satisfy him. He was the living embodiment of that verse from Cavafy:

> *You think now I'll be gone to some city lovelier far than this*
> *could be or ever hope to be...*
> *Don't you see*
> *just as you've ruined your life*
> *in this one spot of ground*
> *you've ruined it over the whole earth*

But in his case it was not ruined – he was a man of great talent – but just unused. Never fulfilled in potential, his dissatisfaction became a canker eating him up. Not a day goes past when I don't think of him – I suppose all men live in the shadow of their fathers. For me it is a warm, if sometimes disapproving, shadow to shelter under.

The road has changed little in 24 years. I pass the great hydro-electric scheme of upper Galloway, generating electricity for the South-west and now blending almost perfectly with the landscape. Soon I am on the moor that fringes the upper reaches of the region, providing a barrier to the visitors that would both enrich and ruin it. And then down into Ayrshire – past Dalmellington, through Patna and into the more fertile and prosperous Ayrshire coastal strip.

Muir came to Ayr a different way – via Gatehouse of Fleet (which he found a 'pleasant secluded little town' but which now is by-passed, yet still full of Muir 'holiday makers' but free now of the feudal arrogance imposed by the late Mrs Murray-Usher who insisted that all the doors of the houses were painted the same colour, even though she didn't own them. Creetown – still flat and surrounded by mud – Newton Stewart (no longer 'clean and handsome', alas, and with more drink licences per head than any other place in Scotland) and then up over the eastern part of the high moor, through Barhill (not so much a one-horse town as a one-railway-station town, for there is little else there) and down to Girvan and on to Maybole.

I have always liked Maybole and the surrounding countryside, not finding in it the symptoms of decay that Muir detected. Quite the reverse in fact, for the coastal and country part of South Ayrshire seems to me to be more traditional and authentically Scottish than much that is more visited. I remember hearing a man from Maybole – admittedly a very old man – talk of 'going for a sail in a car', and discovering that it was a construction still used in parts of South Ayrshire, boats meaning more to them when cars came along than even horse-drawn vehicles.

I worked for a summer in Culzean Country Park, a few miles from Maybole, and although the experience gave me a life-long dislike of the arrogance and elitism of the National Trust for Scotland – a dislike I discovered years later was shared by most ex-employees – I remember that summer with affection. For the first time I came into contact with the pleasure of making sound and pictures work together when I constructed the audio-visual programmes for the planned visitor centre and I recall the joy of being out of doors working with groups of people and helping them to understand and love a place of superlative beauty.

From Maybole it is a green and winding journey to Ayr, and one that no longer has to take the traveller past Burns' birthplace which Muir discovered 'amid a huddle of dusty bungalows and villas' and which, after his visit to the massively over-crowded Burns' Cottage at Alloway, he described as being 'one of the most ludicrous and pathetic sights in Scotland'. In one of his rare forays into prophesy, Muir set to wondering 'how the management will deal with this enormous traffic in another fifty years time...the cottage will certainly have to be enlarged or else the price of admission raised until only the well-to-do can get in. There seems no third alternative except demolition'.

But there was. There are now other places to visit as well as the cottage – a Burns' Centre, the Alloway Kirkyard, and signs direct you to the Brig where Meg, of *Tam o'Shanter* fame, lost her tail. There is the Burns Monument too, and a hotel of the same name not a stone's throw from it. Instead of just the cottage it is a little 'Burnsville' and although it can be crowded it can also be almost deserted. It may even be that the number of tourists is actually less than it was – perhaps now it is Wonderworld, with pools and amusements at the Heads of Ayr that is a greater draw, and that it is that sort of place in which the crowds that would draw Muir's censure as the inevitable product of a 'commercialised, newspaper-reading, bus-driven, cinema-educated age' now gather – or the 21st-century equivalent, that would have to mention car driving, satellite television and video watching.

Muir's visit to Burns' Cottage – after his spleen about the crowds is exhausted – set him thinking also about the myth-making propensity of the Scots. 'The history of Scotland', he writes, 'is filled with legendary figures, actual characters on which the popular imagination has worked, making them its own and by so doing transfiguring them. Wallace and Bruce, Mary Stuart and Prince Charlie are not so much historical characters as figures in an unwritten ballad: they have taken on an almost purely poetical reality...'

Later 20th-century historical revisionism has therefore done us a great service. When I think of Wallace and Bruce, Mary Stuart and Prince Charlie – when I think of Burns – it is much more likely to be coloured by what modern historians have taught us, and about the warts and all which we see in those figures. Wallace – even in the *Braveheart* version – has a dirty face and some unpleasant personal habits. Bruce – especially in *Braveheart* – makes his way by trimming and political subterfuge, until he discovers that honesty pays better dividends. And now modern pathology and scholarship has even revealed his face to us at last, one which is largely disfigured by leprosy and which is unlikely to find its way on to one of our pound notes.

Mary Stuart was feckless and obstinate; Charles Edward Stuart became an alcoholic who drowned his failure in a 'minch of sherries', in the memorable phrase of Ian Crichton Smith. So it goes on – humanity has entered into history, and made our past more relevant by revealing the people in it as people. But it is not history as soap opera, as the grandest critics complain. It is history that lets us appreciate all the more the workings that have brought us here. For a Mary Stuart with diplomatic skills might have changed the course of British politics, and a Charles Stuart who believed in more than dressing up and his divine right to the British throne might have got further than Derby and been forced to concede the restoration of the Scottish Parliament which so many of his supporters wanted (though about which he seemed somewhat disinterested).

Nor does such history diminish an appreciation of real achievement. Muir is right to praise Burns' 'keen and sure moral sense' and to admire not the jolly ploughman become poet, but a man who had a life 'filled with misery and disappointment, which he bore bravely'. The fact that he was a poor manager and unequal to the challenge of subsistence farming does not diminish our admiration for him – if anything it increases it. And as with Burns so with Bruce (in whom low politics and ambition became high statecraft by force of personality and dint of deep self-examination) and with many others. If a historical figure is diminished by knowing at a distance his or her weaknesses or mistakes: by knowing what made the man or woman what they were – then that figure does not deserve the position that a less exhaustive historical method once found for him or her.

Muir came to Ayr depressed by his experience of Burns and Burnsiana. It was, he said 'a pleasant country town imprisoned among suburbs which had been lifted complete from Glasgow and set down on every side'. The suburbs now are almost towns in themselves, and, as is the case everywhere else, they too have grown excrescences, acres of look alike modern villas to suit every price range, and many of the more average tastes. But Ayr at its heart is still a pleasant town – though massively crowded now, and with a pedestrianised High Street whose rows of chain stores and building societies have robbed it of the variegated charm of the 1960s, when my father briefly owned a shop at the top end, where I used to while away school holidays in the back office, or childishly help assistants whose names I have long forgotten.

Today I am stopping in Ayr to talk to a friend who is still in the Labour party, whose name I shall not give for being a friend of mine will not help him in today's political world. From time to time I meet him in various parts of Scotland and we joust about our respective positions. This afternoon, though, he is worried – he brings news that Labour is concerned about what they see as a rise in SNP support: the number crunchers have been at work on local by–elections and polls and think there is a trend developing in our favour.

His attitude to the SNP has always been dismissive, but I catch a whiff of something else now. Perhaps it is the fear that the much vaunted devolution policy will not after all 'kill the Nationalists stone dead', as prophesied by the hapless George Robertson, once Shadow Secretary of State and now Defence Secretary. Neither of us are aware that the coming months have much more of that sort of worry for Labour in store.

We have a cup to tea in a soulless café and we discuss (again) his problems with nationalism. It is easy to dismiss out of hand the misrepresentations, but much harder to make headway against the logical and clear objection that he has. Put simply he wants to see everyone do well – not just the Scots, or the English. He believes that the SNP has a positive role in drawing attention to things that are wrong, but rejects entirely taking my type of politics any further. 'Internationalism not nationalism', he keeps saying. But I am internationalist too, I keep responding. I am keen to base my future on an openness to the world which I do not find in any Westminster party. Our new parliament can start that process.

It can't, he says. It should be a level of subsidiarity, taking appropriate local and regional decisions, but letting the wider ones be made on a larger platform. He still believes in Britain, in the Union of the Parliaments, and in the partnership on which the United Kingdom was built, and he believes in them with a high-minded consistency which I find admirable, although I don't agree with the conclusions he draws from it. He thinks that devolution will work positively to strengthen the Union. 'But only', he adds with accurate prescience, 'if Labour – even New Labour – keeps its promises and pays attention to what Scotland wants. If it doesn't then you are likely to be going far.' Yet he says it in a way that makes clear he regards that possibility as less than welcome.

We part as the clouds gather again. His politics of principle sit unhappily now in a party to which opportunism and populism is a way of life. But it is vitally important to be able to respect at least some of your political opponents, for the first step to totalitarianism is the step that demonises all those with whom one does not agree.

I escape Prestwick – which Muir (with what is beginning to seem like simple bad temper on this part of his journey) called 'a glaring concrete waste' – by taking the by-pass, and although the signs beckon me, as they do every time I am here, I deliberately drive past my old home town of Troon, saving the journey for another day. In any case I have not yet made arrangements to visit my old school, Marr College, and I want to meet pupils there and see what they want from their country and their new democracy. So I content myself with a leisurely drive up the Ayrshire coast on my way to get the ferry home to Argyll.

I had expected to return to Troon quite quickly, but – to keep the Burns' theme going – 'the best laid plans of mice and men gang aft aglay'. Some weeks after driving past the 'green dome' of Marr College I wrote to the Rector asking if I might visit the school, see round and talk to a group of senior pupils. I even enclosed a copy of my last book as a gift for the school library, and to stress my good intentions. Answer came there none. Weeks passed, and all sorts of work intervened. I started to write up this book, leaving this chapter aside until I had made my visit. In early June I wrote again, stressing that the matter was now urgent and then – as there was still no reply – I phoned to seek an answer. Eventually I made it past the school secretaries and found Mr Bone, the Rector, in his office. But after a few moments he asked if I was the 'SNP Michael Russell'. As I had made no secret of it, and indeed believed that I had made it clear, I admitted it. 'Ah then', he sighed, 'you will have to ask the Director of Education if you can come to the school and talk to anyone.'

He gave me the name of the Director of Education, a Mr McCabe who dwelt in the lofty towers of the Council Buildings in Ayr. Now, with time running out, I faxed Mr McCabe. Then I rang Mr McCabe. Then I rang Mr McCabe again. Each time he was 'in a meeting' or 'out of the office'. I had set aside a morning for the visit when I was due to be in Ayrshire talking to Councillors about the extraordinary failures of the Labour-controlled neighbouring East Ayrshire Council, which lost over £3 million on its Direct Labour Organisation. That came and went, though I did drive out to the village of Knockentiber to see the place where both my paternal grandparents came from. It was a soulless place, with a disproportionately large council housing estate and a renovated pub 'The Tiber Inn' which looked as if it might foam with much blood on a Friday night.

A week passed. I rang again – this time from Winnie Ewing's office in the European Parliament in Strasbourg, where I was spending two days. Mr McCabe was still not in. 'But', said his secretary, 'I think he has written to you'. I asked what he had said. 'It's in the letter,' she replied gnomically.

Three days later a refusal arrived. More than a refusal, it

charged me with having misled Mr Bone about my political activities. It implied I had tried to fool him, so that I could gain access to young minds. Thus I could not be allowed to talk to any pupils – or rather I could only talk to any pupils if I was part of an all party event. Obviously no such event was planned.

However Mr McCabe was keen not to be seen as an unreasonable man. I could visit the school and be shown it by Mr Bone. Presumably his presence would make certain I did not so much as glance at a child, in case they were transfixed with some political brainwashing rays from my eyes.

My first reaction to Mr McCabe's response was unprintable. I had not only been a pupil at Marr College, as I had made clear to Mr Bone, so had both my brothers, my two cousins, my aunt and – most importantly of all – my father. Indeed I was so keen to talk to some pupils because my father had been in the first-ever intake of pupils to the school in 1935 – the year that Muir's book appeared. I wanted to measure what I knew of my father's contemporaries and what had happened to them, with those I had been at school with, and with the attitudes of today's generation. I had explained that to Mr Bone and Mr McCabe. It had made no difference.

I was tempted to see a deep political plot in Mr McCabe's actions. After all, South Ayrshire is a Labour authority – almost New Labour – and the school lies in a Labour constituency. Perhaps there was an element of that reasoning in his decision, and perhaps also (this was more likely) because Mr McCabe is a product of the old Strathclyde Region Education Department (a one-party fiefdom if ever there was one), there would be an inbuilt nervousness about the SNP.

But more likely it was just bureaucratic inertia, the fear of doing anything, in case something untoward comes of it. Safer by far to have a blanket ban on politics in schools, save if it is sanitised in Modern Studies classes. Above all do not apply rules in a sensible way – even by asking me to ensure that my conversations were non-political, which (believe it or not) politicians can do!

My choice was now to abandon the visit, or go with the limited purpose of at least seeing the school. I chose the latter, but it was still not plain sailing. I rang Mr Bone – but by now it was the start of the last week of term. He was interviewing all week: perhaps I could come next week. I pointed out that I wanted to see the school with some children in it, no matter how few. He relented – I could visit on the last morning of term: 'Come at nine, double-park outside and I'll give you a cup of coffee', he said. It had taken over four months to get the invitation.

As the day approaches, I almost cancel. For years I have had a recurrent low-level nightmare about being in the school (Room 5 to be precise), and realising that I have done no work and cannot hope to pass my exams. I have never re-visited since I left, and never go to the reunions that the keener former pupils used to invite the less keen to: in fact I don't even get the invitations any more. I am not a fan of the 'alma mater' syndrome and perhaps there are better ways to measure what is happening than to compare it to what used to happen. But curiosity and the oddest feeling of affection for the school – not a feeling I had ever had before – persuade me to take advantage of the hard-won concession from the education authority.

It was 9.20 and raining when I turned up. I had dithered getting dressed, aware of butterflies in my stomach at going back to a place I had not set foot in since 1970. I also had my father on my mind, and at the last minute put on his gold cuff links from the box on the dressing table. The ferry taking me across the Clyde was also late, and that was compounded by road works and commuting traffic.

Outwardly the school has not changed a lot. One still takes a dangerous and blind right turn at the top of a railway bridge, and then the drive sweeps past impressive stone pillars and under an avenue of trees. The natural barrier of the railway line on the left is no longer there – replaced by a wide tract of scrubby grassland – nor is the private footbridge that took generations of pupils out of the grounds to gather round a small general store that sold individual cigarettes.

I park opposite the front door – on the other side of the oval lawn, surrounded by small stone walls. As I bustle up the front steps I am astonished to meet two pupils coming out the main door: strictly forbidden in my day except on the last day of term, but then I recall this is the last day of term. The impressive stone entrance hall – the ground floor of a circular tower that is topped by the green copper dome – contains at its centre a plinth with the bust of Charles Kerr Marr, the Troon coal merchant who gave his fortune to educate the youth of his home town. This hall at one time was bare of everything else – a sort of funerary shrine for Marr himself, like an East German mausoleum. Now, however, it resembles a junk room, with display cases, banners and even old boxes in the corners. It is an overcrowded sign of things to come.

The old building of the school (opened in 1935) consists of two squares on three levels, joined in the middle by the round (domed) tower at the front with an assembly hall behind it. The entrances for pupils are at each side of the building (boys to the left, girls to the right) with outside toilet blocks at those entrances, as well as a janitor's house by the girls' entrance. To this was added in the late 1970s a large new building on the girls' side, joined to the school by a first-floor glass corridor.

The public office is still where it was, but the Rector's office – which was next to it – has been moved to the old medical room. I am taken to a waiting area beside the hall (partitioned from the two galleries that at one time served as museum and exhibition space – some of the artefacts still lie about, and I find myself sitting next to a Schulz bust of Sir Alexander Walker) but very quickly Mr Bone arrives and shows me into his study. It is cluttered with books, memorabilia and assorted other items. He has a small kettle and makes me a cup of coffee whilst we talk.

The entrance hall and the waiting area have given me substantial clues to the problems he starts to outline. A school built for 400 pupils now accommodates almost 1400. Even with the new building, it is bursting at the seams. The school handbook he gives me outlines the numbers – there is pictorial evidence in the wall in his study containing the group portraits of school prefects since 1935. I quickly find my father in the first picture – about a dozen teenagers in the school uniform of purple and gold, that first-ever intake, whose looks of awe at where they found themselves are suprisingly well preserved. I find my picture in the 1969/70 final year – more than two dozen in this one, and all the sixth year became prefects then. Now there are 191 pupils in the sixth year.

More than a third of the children in the school are there on placing requests – ferried in by their parents from Irvine or Prestwick, because Marr College is meant to be a good school. The remaining two thirds – almost 800 pupils – come from Troon, Barassie, Muirhead, Loans and Dundonald, from five feeder primaries that service a commuter conglomeration that has doubled in size in the last 20 years.

I am given the latest school prize list, and the sixth form handbook (Mr Bone is proud of the fact that he has allowed himself to be caricatured in its introduction). I begin to feel that Mr Bone is treating me like the court of history, feeling that I am there to judge him and his stewardship of what he keeps calling 'a school with a great tradition'. It is equally obvious that he feels overwhelmed by the problems that such a school has given him – he confides that he intends to retire at 60, and that he is the first Rector of the school to have come from the same post at another Ayrshire secondary. He is also only the fifth Rector in the school's history.

The scale of his problems becomes obvious the moment he starts to take me on a guided tour. The magnificent library (the first floor of the dome) is full of cheap imitation leather lounging seats – it has become an additional staff room. The boardroom just below the dome – the scene of small exams and rarefied Trust meetings when I was at school – is a junk room, with the specially made furniture casually tossed to one side. It is not even used for school board meetings. The corridors – wood-panelled – are decaying, with rotting metal window frames. The brightest and best equipped rooms are in the old dining hall, which has been partitioned, painted and adapted to house business studies and a whole bank of new computers. In Room 1– the home of Latin 30 years ago – a rickle of pupils is huddled round a teacher in what looks like Victorian squalor.

We cross the walkway to the new building. Despite its design, it is little better – cracked and torn floor coverings, peeling paint in the narrow corridors, with only an inspired art department, well-equipped sports halls and a neat library to commend it. The snack bar and the cafeteria are dank and unpleasant. Mr Bone is fighting a losing battle against numbers and decay. He may be fighting it as well as he can, but he is losing at the moment. And he knows it.

He explains that the Council architects have already spent £300,000 on stabilising the structure. They need to spend another £3 million to make it good, but such money is hard to come by. He 'expects' the restoration to start soon. The old building is still owned by the Marr Trust, the body that administers what remains of Charles Kerr Marr's legacy. They have built a new sports pavilion in recent years, but they show little interest in contributing to the upkeep of the school building. That burden falls on South Ayrshire Council.

When Marr College opened in 1935 it was one of the most modern, best-equipped school buildings in Scotland. Teachers were on an enhanced pay scale, in order to attract the best. Whilst it was being constructed a stream of distinguished visitors were shown this showpiece of Scottish educational achievement – including Ribbentrop, then the Nazi Ambassador to London, who had been a wine merchant and who knew Sir Alexander Walker (of Johnnie Walker fame), by that time Chairman of the School Governors. Charles Kerr Marr wanted the building to be magnificent – both to emphasise the importance of education, and to give the children of his home-town the best start in life. He recognised that the *mens sana* needed a healthy building too.

Even in the late 1960s, the physical fabric was impressive.

The school had grant maintained status, getting money from the government but also using the Marr Trust resources. It was a true comprehensive, taking children from the town of Troon without regard to their abilities, and giving them the equal opportunity of a good education. When grant aid was abolished, and when Strathclyde Region took over the school, it was Strathclyde that provided a well-designed, modern extension so that the school could continue to have the best possible facilities. It seemed as if the tension between what the old Ayrshire County Council had regarded as a 'rival' in education in Ayrshire (they had a representative on the Trust, because they had been required to put a small amount of money into the school to guarantee its completion during a difficult period for the Marr Trust) was at an end, and that the school could continue to flourish as part of the state system. It could have, had the state system flourished. But it hasn't, because state education has been mismanaged and starved of resources for all of the past 20 years.

So now what was a fine school building is overcrowded, dilapidated and still declining. Educational standards don't seem to have slipped too much yet – the school has a record of academic achievement and sporting prowess that Mr Bone is justly proud of: even in sports like basketball, that would have been shunned 20 years ago. Their basketball guru – coaching teams that win the all-Scotland prizes – is also the head of business studies, with that well-ordered, attractive department.

But, back in his study, Mr Bone admits that the last HMI report was not all it could have been – he hints at his agenda to change things, as if he has met untoward resistance so far. 'I quickly learnt here that the management tools I used at my former school just won't do', he say plaintively. 'But things have slipped and they can be improved.'

He denies a link between overcrowding, run-down buildings and that slippage. But as another former Strathclyde employee, he is better at the jargon of constant educational 'improvement' than he is at analysis of his problems – or perhaps such analysis is just not permitted to be voiced. I leave him after an hour and half. I have the impression of a man desperately keeping the lid on a boiling pot – a pot of decay and decline that he is powerless to cool down. Powerless not because he is incapable of leadership and advocacy of this once great school, but because the culture of leadership and advocacy has been bred out of his generation of head teachers. They are there to cope, not to change.

I get his permission to walk out through the boys entrance – the outside toilets have been refurbished (but they are locked between lessons!) and indeed are no longer outside, because the immediate area has been glassed in and roofed. I stand at the spot where we used to stand everyday at break time (our spot – every group had them) and realise I am angry: angry at what has happened here in the past 30 years.

What happened to the belief in constant improvement – in things getting better because society wanted to change and improve? I am sure those I was at school with believed in it, and I am equally sure that my father's generation believed in it too – indeed in the classic phrase, they 'fought for it in a world war', or something like it. But things have not got better – and there is now a resignation about that fact, especially in the places (such as in the Rector's study) where such resignation is fatal.

Education is the foundation of society – and if we don't resource education, then we don't invest in our future. Perhaps we are not yet at the absolute crisis, but the signs of crisis are already all around. Crumbling buildings, overcrowded schools, not enough materials or books to go round – ask any teacher and they will tell you about these facts of life. And those same teachers will be working towards their retirement – tired of the constant struggle, and exhausted by having to make do. Educational administrators can parrot what they like – can bamboozle councillors, resist outside scrutiny and pretend that all is well, and that they are managing despite the cuts and the compromises. They can close schools and welcome fake government initiatives that are the merest window dressing. They can even (disgracefully) play along with politicians who try to shift the blame on to so-called 'failing teachers' when society should be targeting 'failing politicians', 'failing administrators' and 'failing Directors of Education'.

But what they can't do is hide the decline forever. The Tory mantra that you can't solve problems by throwing money at them – the Tory mantra that New Labour has made their theme tune – is quite untrue in terms of education. You will only solve the problem of education – you will only provide the base for building – if you invest more in upgrading schools, provide good learning environments and give teachers the chance to teach in decent, well-resourced, surroundings. What's more, such investment will pay as many spin-off dividends as building one frigate or one submarine. Jobs in design, building, refurbishment and maintenance; jobs in academic publishing and IT, and teaching jobs which are attractive to graduates, not the last resort.

Driving back out along the avenue of trees I see a pupil walking my way. I stop and he looks at me suspiciously. I am going to break my parole and ask him what he thinks of his school.

'All right', he says. What 'all right', how 'all right', why 'all right', I ask. 'All right, but it would be good if they cleaned it up a bit'. Will the new parliament do it? I suggest. 'Doubt it', he says, 'there's not enough money'.

But shouldn't there be?

'Yes. But there isn't'.

Propaganda has got through to him (as well as to, or perhaps from, Mr Bone, Mr McCabe and the rest of the educational Mafia), even in one of the richest nations in the world.

Education, education, education. If it means anything it means starting on treating education seriously in the new parliament, and persuading people that ignorance is much more expensive than knowledge.

'The very poor', observed Muir when talking about the decayed housing and slums he saw in Kilmarnock and then in

Glasgow, 'are almost more hard to convert to Socialism than the very rich, it is true: partly because they are too sunk in hopelessness to open their minds to an idea'. Now we have a society that is hard to convert to a new hope about the future, because so much has failed them before. As it was, so it will be. But there are better things to spend money on than nuclear weapons and tax concessions for the richest. There are things that must be afforded if we are to become the society we have the potential to be.

I drive about Troon for another hour, stopping here and there to measure change in my inner barometer, if I can. St Ninian's Church – where I spent so many hours as a child – is much the same and in the dark stillness of the building I walk up the nave and spend a moment or too sitting in the choir stalls. And then I go and sit in the priest's stall and a whole life that I planned passes before me – an appropriate reaction since it was here that I started to hear my call to the church, no matter how unfulfilled that ultimately turned out to be (at least for the present). I leave the church and go walkabout in the town, looking – in vain as it turns out – for familiar faces who I can importune to tell me about what has happened to them.

Later that night I dream about the school again. And again I am about to fail my exams! But this time the school is as derelict as it actually is today, and has enlarged to accommodate the new building.

My dreams are updating themselves with the reality of modern Scotland.

Chapter Five
Lanarkshire

There is something dirty about Lanarkshire roads. Even the country lanes have a sort of grimy edge to them, as if all sorts of dirt and debris have been swept to the side and are mounting up to be the foundation for the stunted, greyish grass that grows along the verges. In places there are acres upon acres of this grassland – unhealthy looking, scattered at random with dips and puddles. It takes no leap of imagination to surmise that underneath these fields lies the detritus of the industrial revolution, decayed and collapsed but lurking just below the soil like the ruins of a pre-nuclear holocaust civilisation.

Things were worse, though, in 1934. Muir went 'between pocked fields through which iron coloured brooks sluggishly oozed and where stringy gutta-percha bushes rose from sward that looked as if it had been dishonoured by some recondite infamy'. He claimed to notice, in his open-topped car, no 'scents from the hedges and fields' between Glasgow and Hamilton, Airdrie and Motherwell. 'It was', he said, 'as if in this region nature no longer breathed, or gave out at most the chill dank mineral breath of coal and iron'.

The towns, he claimed were 'like villages on a nightmare scale, which after endless building had never managed to produce what looked like a street and had no centre of any kind. One could not say that these places were flying asunder, for there was no visible sign of anything holding them together: the houses merely stood side by side, of every shape and size they crowded upon each other so hard that they seemed to be squabbling in a slatternly, apathetic dejected way for their places'. He was no more complementary about the villages. They looked 'like dismembered parts of towns brutally hacked off, and with the raw edges left nakedly exposed.'

This 'wilderness of grime, coal-dust and brick, under a blackish grey synthetic sky', these 'bloated and scabbed villages' with their 'ranges of slag heaps, miniature mountain ranges which…give the illusion of being geological in formation' have, to be charitable, changed for the better. The houses squabbling for places have long since been swept away, to be replaced by the dull uniformity of council housing, which is in itself now giving way to more imaginative and human re-designs which bring colour and variety to some of the schemes – though there is much still to be done. And private housing is springing up like uniformly designed mushrooms wherever there is a pocket of land reclaimed from industry.

Lanarkshire of course is really two counties, with a border zone between them. In the north there are the remains of industrial Scotland, stretching from Airdrie and Coatbridge across to the New Town of East Kilbride. In the south are the farming and commuting towns of Biggar and Lanark, and the rolling hills that rise up to Scotland's second-highest village at Leadhills. Between these two highly dissimilar areas is a band of towns and villages like Overtown, Ashgill, Larkhall and Stonehouse which are neither one thing or the other – with the worst of the north slowly giving was to the gentler, more countrified south.

For nine years I lived at the bottom edge of this border zone – in the fictionally named Tillietudlem, a rickle of a dozen or so houses on the edge of a hill. The name comes from 'Tillietudlem Castle', in Scott's *Old Mortality*, based – some say

– on the real Craignethan Castle which lies behind the village. The houses that are left are the foreman's and manager's from a pit that was opened in the Castle grounds in the late 19th century, and closed within 50 years. The railway halt – complete with Tillietudlem station signboards – went a decade later even before the Beeching cuts. The pit bing was taken away in the 1970s to provide bottoming for the new A74 as it spread out and down towards England. All that was left were the houses and some fields – and the curious name that always got a response when you had to give it in shops or offices.

I stood for parliament in this constituency – Clydesdale, running from Elvanfoot in the deep south of Lanarkshire north to Larkhall on the top of the border zone, and east from distant Dolphinton (really in the Borders) to Stonehouse, which was meant to be the site of the last New Town in Scotland, but which got bogged down in planners' blight and ended up with nothing. That election – the 1987 General Election – seems a political age away. At the height of the Nigel Lawson boom, Scotland was still doggedly behind Labour, but Labour was well behind the Tories and no matter what the Scots did, it was the Tory vote in England that would count. I trudged the countryside and the towns, shaking hands, knocking on doors and – fired with enthusiasm – fell prey to the disease known as candidate-itis: the belief that were circumstances in which I could win. (It is a common complaint that afflicts candidates in every election, particularly those who are 'also rans'. I have had otherwise sensible men and women pleading with me for extra resources for their campaigns on the grounds that the breakthrough was near, and who, a week later, admit that their hysteria was completely unjustified. That lesson is all the harder learned at an electoral count, when they weigh the Labour vote, as your piles seem to be growing down the way, not up.) However, my secret musings went, if Labour's new would-be MP was really unpopular, if the Alliance (as it then was) was imploding, if the Tories were hated...then I could squeeze through. And everyone was so nice, supportive, friendly...

I came last, with just of 14% of the vote, narrowly passed by the Social Democrat who had spent a fortune and convinced himself even more than me that he would win. His wife was in tears at the count and the good folk of Clydesdale sent Jimmy Hood – the larger than life ex-miner but a heavyweight only in the physical sense – to the Commons. The Tory was still second in those days, and their candidate – a Modern Studies teacher who some described as having a smarmy manner – moved on to work for the Conservatives in the North-east of Scotland, to become an MP at the next election and a Scottish Office minister within two years. Now Raymond Robertson is the chairman of a party with no parliamentary representation in Scotland, no councils in its control and with no Euro MPs. But his manner still appears to be the same and he is still trying to climb the greasy pole.

I won just two areas at the ballot box: New Lanark, the refurbished 'model village' of David Dale and Robert Owen, and a council house estate in Larkhall where I had worked with the tenants' association to try and get their local Labour-controlled council to improve their dreadful and dilapidated housing conditions. I didn't even win my own village, or at least I think I didn't. Of the 12 houses from the corner to the top of the brae I immediately had to discount the farm and the farmer's sister's cottage, since the inhabitants were of some sect that believed voting was sinful. Four out of 23 votes spoiled. Another six votes were dyed-in-the-wool, middle-class professional Labour – the type who were voting Tory in their droves south of the Border, but who in Scotland thought the revolution of peace and justice could still come by means of a Socialist government as long as it was resistant to dancing with duchesses. Of the 13 that remained two were solidly SNP (me and my wife), and six were Tory (though one of those never voted). As this included our closest friends and neighbours it was a bit galling, but had to be tolerated. That left five swing voters.

Our other neighbours (and equally good friends) seemed converted to the SNP and despite the rigours of having to appear on a television clip with me pretending to canvass them as if I didn't know who they were, they still backed me. The remaining three refused to be drawn, went to the polling station and could look me in the eye forever after. But that doesn't mean anything in politics or village life. A straw poll now is somewhat different. For a start the village has grown, with three new houses. Half the previous residents have left but a mental survey of those who have stayed suggests more SNP voters, no Tories at all and perhaps only one die-in-the-ditch Labour voter.

Such a survey of course gives an artificial importance to politics. Living in Tillietudlem for nine years I can think of only one other person in the village who had ever been a member of a political party – and he was lapsed Labour. The frequent village parties talked about everything but the political situation and my own activities were regarded as a reasonably harmless aberration, akin to an obsession with growing orchids or collecting stamps. Politics is a minority sport for all but the obsessed and the obsessive, and it is good for politicians to remember that from time to time.

1987 was a year in the middle of Scotland's last democratic ice age. It was pre-Constitutional Convention, when the cause of a parliament for Scotland was still at a low ebb, sustained by as many principled volunteers as actions by full time politicians. And as the Thatcherite 'loadsamoney' revolution swept England, Scotland seemed to retreat into its shell, knowing passionately that it was agin it, but confused about what it was actually for. From South Lanarkshire the picture was bleak enough – from the industrial north of the county it was akin to Siberia. The awful inevitability of the closure of Scotland's last major steel plant, Ravenscraig, rolled on through the 80s making Motherwell resemble a town on the Western Front, waiting for the final barrage. I spent many a cold hour outside the gates of the steel mill at Gartcosh, protesting at the butchering of the country, and supporting brave but futile campaigns such as the steelworkers' march to London.

For not only were the streets of the capital not paved with

gold, or even steel, but there were bigger political fish to fry at Westminster and Labour wouldn't even push the issue in the House of Commons, preferring to try (and fail) to remove Thatcher in a row over military helicopters. The steel men came home disillusioned. Industrial closure after industrial closure echoed around Scotland and all the big ideas and the big corporate investments of the 60s and 70s went up in smoke (usually quite literally, their sites bulldozed for shopping centres, private housing or to add the to bank of derelict, unused, brownfield land). The Proclaimers captured it beautifully in their song at that time, *Letter from America...*

Bathgate no more
Linwood no more

Walking the streets of Motherwell or Hamilton on a Saturday afternoon in any winter of the late 1980s it was hard not to echo that sentiment and spread it over the whole of what had been Scotland's economic powerhouse. And because industry and economics is about people, the feeling of failure was palpable. The air was full of stale cigarette smoke, the shops specialised in cheap and gaudy goods, poor health and weedy, shallow complexions were everywhere. And political choice was one word – Labour.

When things are bad – and they were bad – then experimentation and untried solutions are less and less attractive. Atavistic hitting out was OK – this town, after all had returned the first every SNP MP, the redoubtable Robert MacIntyre, at a by election in 1945 – but it had reverted to Labour within months at a general election. Just across the motorway, the neighbouring town of Hamilton had given the SNP its first significant victory of modern times in 1967 when Winnie Ewing declared, 'Stop the world, Scotland wants to get on'. She too lost to Labour at the subsequent general election. Now when the axe hovered over every company, and every job, it was to Labour that people still looked – Labour to bind up the wounds, Labour to speak up for Scotland, Labour to bring back the glory days.

And no matter how much people had to take, they still believed that Labour could build the new Jerusalem. Industrial closures and mass unemployment had been experienced before and there was still a shred of hope in a final solution and in a just and more equal society. It was those beliefs that had made me a member of the Labour Party in 1972, whilst still at university, and I could understand the endless stream of voters who – though with less and less certainty as the years passed – would shake off the proffered leaflet or the attempted conversation with the words 'We're Labour, son'.

'There's no gain without pain' said the Tories at Westminster (a British equivalent of John Updike's observation that 'those who tell you how to act always have whisky on their breath') but there just seemed to be no gain here. Of pain there was plenty, but nothing to show for it.

Yet things did change. Despite, rather than because of, the closures, the dole, their world being turned upside down, people went on and found new jobs (mostly created in the sunrise industries) and money was found to start cosmetic surgery on the landscape and townscapes. It was a bit of a hit and miss affair – concrete new brutalism was the architectural style for far too long – but today most people are better off than they were then, living in better houses and with better shops to go to, and with more money to spend in them. Standing in the same shopping precinct in Motherwell it has shed at least a layer of its grimy poverty and the sun does seem to break through from time to time. There are brighter faces and a stronger willingness to stand and talk, and think about the future.

I am in random sample mode today and in half an hour have spoken to six Labour supporters, six SNP and one Tory. The Labour and SNP preferences are almost interchangeable but it is the 'Scottishness' of the party that seems to win out – even the Labour voters are sceptical about Blair and London and are keen to talk about what Scotland can do now. Only two of them take that reference to being speculation about the World Cup.

But get off party politics and the perspectives shift. One or two want the parliament to be here rather than in Edinburgh – or at least somewhere in the West. Independence isn't frightening but there is a feeling that its time is still to come. The majority have little time for politicians, but much more for the fresh start that the parliament might provide. The SNP voters tend to be a bit more apologetic than their Labour counterparts, acknowledging – with one exception – that they have always voted Labour before. But Labour hasn't changed things enough for them: it's all too much as it was. And that seems a bad thing for everyone. Certainly what was in Motherwell was bad. And the Tories take the blame for it, and will do for years. But the comparative affluence is not a year old – it has been growing for at least five years. So either government has nothing to do with prosperity, or the Tories in some strange way did produce gain from the pain, yet will never be thanked for their savage efforts.

I have heard this argument advanced by several Tory apologists in the media (they are more represented there than in any democratic institution!) as a reason for Scotland to overcome its aversions and learn to love the boy Hague. But there may be – indeed probably are – other reasons for the recovery of Scotland. One of those is Europe, and the growth in Scottish manufacturing and exporting. Another is the ability of Scots to take a hammering and bounce back. And a third may lie in the effect of the depression of the 80s – a change in mindset and a determination to build a different country, no longer dependent upon dogma and policy whims at Westminster.

One would have thought that poverty was a great leveller, a shared experience in adversity that would bring disparate parts of the community together. But the opposite often happens. Skinheads and far right parties flourish in the poorer regions of the former East Germany: ghetto violence is common in France and the Unites States. And here at the extremes of poverty in the late 19th and early 20th centuries some, but fortunately not all, took up the tribal weapons to attack, humiliate and subject those from other religious traditions.

As recently as the 1920s the police invoked the public order acts at Carfin to stop Catholics processing to their shrine, and broke a few heads at the mildest objections. By all accounts the actions were approved not just by the authorities, but also by neighbouring working-class Protestants in areas where the Orange Order still holds some sway. Muir turned off his road in Lanarkshire to visit the grotto at Carfin and writes of the testament to faith that it gives. Today it is a peaceful, even holy place – if a little garish for my tastes, though incorporating a lovely modern chapel dedicated to the victims of the Lockerbie air disaster.

Scottish sectarianism still exists, but now in smaller and smaller pockets – and in less and less hearts and minds of inadequates who fear for their own toe hold in society, and therefore try and keep anyone else's toes off the ladder of progress! At one time though sectarianism disfigured parts of Scottish local government, was institutionalised in public appointments and in some private firms, and destroyed faith in the democratic process.

But to give credit where credit is due Labour has been historically successful in blending the two traditions in its party without forcing any side to make a concession or compromise – and it is certainly declining in importance. But if there were to be another catastrophic economic downturn, another depression and the 'sunset of the sunrise', it would be important to have at least a weather eye open for those who might again try and scrape ascendancy in order to protect their position.

I should drive up to Airdrie, or Shotts or some such place and renew my acquaintance with areas that loom darkly in my memories of the worst of Scotland. Perhaps I would be pleasantly surprised and discover that the worst seems to be over. Perhaps I would find a landscape that is healing from the wounds of careless industry and even more careless industrialists. I would certainly find a Muslim community with shops and restaurants and a view that racism – whilst it exists – is substantially less of a problem than it was in Bradford or Leeds where many have come through on their long journey from Pakistan or Bangladesh...and communities that are growing together in a way that may leave them inextricably entwined. As long as the descent into darkness can be held off, then there is every reason to believe that these places have gained in wisdom as well as in wealth.

But I need fresh air and – frankly – a bit of non-industrial Scotland. From the high north of Lanarkshire I can escape to the deep south: and it only takes half an hour. Or rather an hour today as increased prosperity has also brought traffic jams. But it gives me time to think a bit more about what has happened here in the last few years.

The road I am on is an example of it. In the mid 1980s the Tories announced their intention of upgrading the A74 (a matter I referred to in Chapter 3). It was meant to take ten years, but is still not finished – the last section is still being put in place. But the intention was good – or was it? Was it designed to make Scottish industry more profitable by easing the transfer of goods, and to make Scotland a more modern place, or was it really only to give the impression that Westminster could still do things of importance, could still be Scotland's friend? Was it a sop for the resolute refusal of four Tory governments to address the real issue of Scotland – the issue of the democratic deficit, the distant governance and policies designed for those who lived in the Tory shires of England? Worse still, was it a bribe to offset the closures and the destruction of our industries, a bribe to make it easier for the Scots to swallow the bitter pill of Thatcherism? Was it even a highway to the brave new world of reality that Thatcher thought she must drag the Scots towards?

The same words used in that crusade are being used now. The Scots, according to some armchair critics, are simply old-fashioned, reluctant to join in the new world of 'globalisation'. They must be made to look forward, to accept what William MacIlvanney called the 'current social orthodoxies' not – as he rightly observed – challenge them. It is the bright 'new' Cool Britannia that beckons this time, and Scotland is still being ungrateful. So a little carrot of public spending here, a bit more of the stick of welfare reform and public cutbacks and, the theory goes, hey presto, the Scots will be driven into the promised land as meek, if not as happy, as lambs to the slaughter.

The problem with this theory, as with many theories about Scotland that emanate from ouwith our borders, is that it is based on a complete misunderstanding of Scotland. Far from being insular and opposed to globalisation, Scots are keener to take part in the world than most of the others with whom they share this island. Poll after poll has shown stronger support for European institutions: Scots have welcomed and competed for inward investment and Scottish manufacturing exports more, and more successfully, than its equivalent competitors south of the Border. What Scotland requires, to finally allow a full participation in the world of the 21st century, is not driven by Blair or propelled by Thatcher – it is simply the democratic structures that put us in charge of our own destiny. And this is not an *ex post facto* justification for constitutional change – its roots lie even further back than Winnie Ewing's cry about getting onto the world. Scottish pamphleteers of the early 20th century were making the same point and seeing constitutional change as a way of taking part. Isolationism is not a product of nationalism in Scotland – it is an inevitable product of the Union, for with the Union we remain at one step distant from the world, with a voice that is always mediated at the top tables.

I am thinking of international contacts in the grandest sense when I get cut up by a thundering Spanish lorry that almost blocks me off from the exit to Abington. You used to be able to turn right from the old dual carriageway up to Leadhills, but now you must use the slip road and negotiate what seem to be myriad roundabouts before starting the long climb to some of Scotland's highest villages. The highest is actually Wanlockhead, which lies just over the county border, in Dumfriesshire. It asserts its right to its lofty accolade jealously – when the village of Dalwhinnie presumed to claim the title on a large sign by the A9 to Inverness, it soon had to alter it to 'Highest village in the Highlands', for Wanlockhead – as the crow flies not much more than 40 miles from the English border – sits above every other township in the land.

Visitors who expect a rural idyll are in for a surprise, though. Leadhills is aptly named – a centre of 18th and 19th century lead mining, along with periodic prospecting for other metals including gold. Royal wedding rings are by tradition made from gold from these Lowther Hills and in the summer it is not uncommon to see figures in the streams, panning for 'instant' riches. I visited Leadhills often when I was the local parliamentary candidate, and each time I seemed to end up standing looking at a lump of old metal, whilst being surrounded by railway enthusiasts who had taken on the Herculean task of starting to restore the railway that ran from the valley of the River Clyde (where the motorway is now) up to the villages. This narrow-gauge system was once used to take lead ore out and to bring in goods and passengers.

Today there are a couple of miles that can actually carry the minuscule carriages that have been dredged from other railways to form the basis of a tourist attraction. The wee diesel train is similarly tiny, and it labours along at about five miles an hour. It is actually faster to walk – at least uphill from Leadhills to Wanlockhead. Gravity assists the train on the way back. The train journey is the precursor to a visit to the leadmine itself – only one has been preserved, along with a restored mine worker's cottage – and a plush visitors' centre, all completed with European money. Resistant as I am to tourist versions of history, there is something moving about the story of the lives of those who once worked here – the hardship for children working from the age of 5, the deaths and maimings for those who went up and down 80-ft shafts standing in a bucket that dangled on a fraying rope, the inevitable lead pollution. And yet they maintained a strong belief in education, in self-improvement and they valued their self-respect.

The mines were owned by Quakers who forbade alcohol or gambling – on pain of dismissal – and hired in labour from as far afield as Cornwall. Their moral standards permitted child labour but perhaps that can be forgiven in the climate of the times. Certainly they did their best to lift the spirits and the minds of those who worked for them, and they were followed in ownership by one of the better lairds in Scotland, the Duke of Buccleuch, who improved the houses and relaxed the rules.

It was the 19th and early 20th century version of globalisation that did for the mines too: the ability to import lead more cheaply, and the gradual exhaustion of profitable seams. But being so far from the markets, these mines had no alternatives and even today Wanlockhead in particular has a down-at-heel appearance – the cosmetic treatment for tourists not even skin deep. I have been here several times before – most recently with a party of 30 or so invited by a close friend as part of his weekend-long celebrations for a 50th birthday. We repaired after our visit for a buffet lunch up at the Jacobean Pub, high above the village. The building housing the bar was intact, if ramshackle – but all around it were the ruins of some larger enterprise that seemed to have been shelled by insurgents. Doors and windows hung out of their frames, and rubble and weeds filled the courtyards.

Inside the bar was Nat-friendly: the walls were covered in tartan, Scottish momentos abounded, broadswords were hung high and a framed Declaration of Arbroath was prominent. We ate game pies and salad, myself quite comfortable amongst familiar talismans, many of the others ill at ease and worried. Miles from anywhere the scene might have been set for a Scottish version of the Deep South tourist terror movie *Deliverance*, when we would be pitted against the dark and frightening forces of restless natives turning against poor, hapless incomers. On the evidence on the walls I would get a ride home, while my very Tory companions might be detained for a while, perhaps never to emerge.

Normally coming this way I would carry on, down through the aforesaid Duke's domain around Thornhill to the prosperous farmlands of Dumfries and then south to the Solway. But I had other places to visit, and this was a detour to get me out of industrial Scotland. Perhaps it was proof that such a journey is not possible in Lanarkshire, so to convince myself I ambled back north by way of Symington, Thankerton, and Lanark – the last mentioned being very much a county farming town, which sits uncomfortably with the industrial heartland that takes its name. Lanark, like Hawick, Gala and Langholm amongst others, has an annual riding of the marches – Lanimers – which is almost a religion to the natives of Lanark. Twice in recent years it has had to be postponed because it clashed with the date of a General Election, and twice there have been dire warnings to the government by Lanarkians.

The whole event is an exercise in conspicuous consumption; cod-history dressed up with 'Maids of Honour', Lord Cornets and all the other spurious trappings of the Border festivals. Lanark's Riding of the Marches was originally a religious event, as all were, and what exists now is a late 19th century sham, which is in the grip a false and overweening small-minded civic pride. Perhaps that is too critical, but it has always annoyed me that the town should celebrate – at best – made-up history while ignoring in great part its genuine past. For Lanark's claim to historical fame lies in quite another direction – a direction indicated by a huge and threatening statue built into the tower of the Parish Church, which dominates the High Street and diverts the traffic flowing out of town.

William Wallace burnt Lanark in revenge for the murder of his wife by the local sheriff in the year 1297. There is a stone just by the church that commemorates the site of his house, and every year a wreath is laid on it by local Nationalists in a ceremony that is attracting more and more community support, but not official support, despite frequent requests. Lanark is genuinely the second oldest Royal Burgh in Scotland but assists no one but the elect in understanding and celebrating its history. It is making very little of so much potential – potential that is being fulfilled in New Lanark, down the hill and into the Clyde Valley which is now recognised as a World Heritage Site and which, in the best way it can, and not without the odd hiccup and false start, is telling a story of social improvement and community concern that should be a lesson for today.

If I am hard on Lanark, it is not because I have no friends there. One of the local GPs, Jamie Hill, is my son's godfather, the doctor in whom I have the most faith and who I consult whenever my hypochondria needs reassurance. Jamie is a great example of how this country is changing – patrician, of Anglican/Episcopal background, happily straddling the social union from which we all come, he has worked his way towards an open and excited view of the future in which it would be quite natural for Scotland to do well independently. And he holds that position despite a set of friends who wave garlic and cross themselves – in a Presbyterian fashion of course – at the merest mention of the SNP.

I have gone further than Muir into Lanarkshire, and I have also come here before visiting Glasgow – the reverse of his journey. I turn down the hill into the Clyde Valley – the centre of Scotland's garden centre industry and the inevitable destination for a 'wee drive out' these days for city families and their 2.4 children. The plum blossom is fading, but there are new plum orchards being planted again, thank goodness and although Clyde Valley tomatoes are not the money spinner they once were (blame the Dutch, my grower friends tell me, for subsidising their gas and driving out the Scottish product) bedding plants and nurseries have plugged into the UK-wide growth in gardening and built themselves into sizeable units in this part of Lanarkshire.

And building imagination as well. One of the most remarkable projects of recent years was the re-creation of Van Gogh's world-famous painting of sunflowers, made entirely of bedding plants, and sitting in the middle of a wheat field in the Borders. The picture – it has to be a called that – was the brainchild of one man, Alastair Scott the son of market gardeners in the Clyde Valley, and himself a grower with a reputation for innovation and eccentric dress: the only post-punk horticulturist in Scotland, if not the world. In the manner of visionaries Alastair bullied, wheedled and (it has to be said) conned most of his colleagues in the business to support his idea, devised how it could be done and had the force of will to take it to fruition, even when the planting in wet weather began to look like an impossible job (hundreds of thousands of plants take a long time to put in the ground!)

I was asked if I would organise the media coverage of the project – unpaid of course. I did, and had the luckiest of escapes when the tabloids decided to search out the field for themselves, finding it by helicopter just as it flowered, revealing the Van Gogh image with a remarkable clarity. Despite Alastair's wish to keep it under wraps for another two days until the official launch date, I persuaded the committee (Alastair had eventually been forced to accept at least a little collective advice) to press release it as soon as it had been seen.

Had we waited, we would have held our press conference on site of the day of the Russian coup! As it was we made the front pages in five continents, and pictures were carried on television from Alaska to Arabia. The image looked even more sensational when it was eventually being ploughed back into the earth – the picture of a tractor slowly eliminating line upon line of it, taken from the air, is one of my favourite images and still sells as a postcard.

Alastair's enthusiasm was not dented by the hard reality of 'sunflowers'. The last time I saw him he was planning an image double the size, this time on a hillside above the Clyde Valley so that it could be seen in its full glory without taking to the air. And being Alastair, this time the picture would be by Andy Warhol.

Scotland has never been short of genuine visionaries – not many, though, are as free-thinking as Alastair, or as uniquely blessed with a medium to work in that is as natural or flexible as good Scottish bedding plants! The first of this year's crop is on sale as I drive along the valley, but there is an even newer crop – commuter housing advertised in every village.

I suddenly look at the road edges and discover that they

are fresh with grass with flowers. Where has my dirty Lanarkshire gone? Is it just prejudice that makes me think of the county in that way, when it has – as I know – so much diversity? As if to question my question I turn down from a sign to Larkhall and join the motorway. There is debris on every side. And that's the way it stays until I reach Glasgow.

Chapter Six
Glasgow

Edinburgh stands above Scotland: Glasgow seems to be part of every other part of the country.

They used to say that if you went to any port anywhere in the world, climbed on board a ship and shouted down into the engine room 'Jock', you would get an answering affirmative shout. Scotland at times seems like that – if you go anywhere, and walk into a bar you will find a Glaswegian sitting in the corner. Or someone who spent his youth in Glasgow, or whose mum, or auntie, or brother lives or works there. It is the industrial magnet for the working class iron in the Scottish soul.

And yet, important as it is, times have changed. Muir's assertion that, 'a description of Scotland which did not put Glasgow in the centre of the picture would not be a description of Scotland at all' could not be justified today. The 'second city of the empire' has shrunk in population and size, and even influence, although it has perhaps grown in positive reputation. And you are as likely to find in a Scottish bar – any Scottish bar – someone who has worked on the rigs, or lived overseas. Glasgow is not any longer at the centre of the Scottish universe.

As a child, growing up on the Ayrshire coast, it was a great day out to take the train to Glasgow. Then it was to the Victorian splendour of St Enoch's Station that the train hurtled (it was even a steam train in the very earliest of those trips) and from there it was a taxi ride to the dentist, or to lunch with a friend of my mother's in some smart but faded restaurant. On occasion the *raison d'être* of the journey was a trip to the theatre with friends or the school (a pantomime, a ballet, even an opera) and these visits might include high tea at some Glasgow emporium, complete with silver-gilt cake stands and floury scones. Sometimes there was Christmas shopping to be done in – what seemed then – the huge space of Frasers department store, with Christmas lights and garish artificial Christmas trees on every level of its vast open halls.

These journeys only occasionally included my father, yet at one time he travelled that way every day, commuting to university as he changed career at the age of 40. He journeyed alongside some of his old school friends, who were still pursuing jobs in Glasgow that they had started when they left school. I suspect my father had had enough of travelling to Glasgow during those years, and always absented himself from my mother's shopping expeditions. In any case, as a family with Edinburgh ties, we tended to visit that city together, not the one nearest us.

St Enoch's station is no more, but on a whim I decide to start my look at Glasgow from where it stood – from the square and the huge glass-roofed pyramid shopping centre that still bears its name.

I stand beside it and can look all the way up Buchanan Street – pedestrianised now – to the Royal Concert Hall and to yet another temple of mammon being built to house yet more shops. There is constant building going on everywhere I look – refurbishment, gap sites being filled, street furniture being renewed or erected. For a city that the press tell us is in the last throes of civic decline, it looks suspiciously prosperous and busy. There are crowds even on a late Thursday afternoon – and why not, for many of them this is still pay day!

To my right, past the huge shopping centre (the largest

glass-roofed structure in Europe, somebody tells me) lies the Merchant City, renewed and renamed as part of the remaking of Glasgow in this decade. It needed remaking, of course. That child who travelled to St Enoch's Station and to the black, sooty buildings that lay beyond it, was fed a diet of fear about Glasgow from anxious parents. Glasgow had gangs (razor gangs – the words were whispered), rickets, slums, drunks (and not just with alcohol in their system), the Gorbals, poverty, crime, hard men and brassy women, and the dirt and detritus of industrialisation everywhere. I suspect my mother never returned to the douce wee station at Troon without a metaphorical thanks to God for being spared that which Glasgow might have thrown at us.

Like most places that have had to contend with decline and decay, Glasgow has also had to cope with a lot of misrepresentation over the years. On the way up it is hard graft and you make enemies: on the way down the enemies gather like a Greek chorus to comment with satisfaction on your decline. So the factory of the world (that made more than half the steam trains ever built, and shipped them from the fine Finnieston crane) became a den of vice and depravity, and Edinburgh pulled in its skirt and clucked at having such a dirty neighbour. My mother believed the Edinburgh stories.

Certainly Glasgow, going up or going down, is very different from the capital. It has a gritty energy and a way of plain speaking that is shocking further east. And I like it for that. Of course Glasgow is not a single unit, a homogeneous whole. More than any other Scottish city it spreads itself over the whole gamut of ways of living and of different communities with different expectations. Its constituent parts are like whole cities in themselves – diverse and diverting. On the South Side you can go from derelict council schemes (the worst of which have since been bulldozed and blown up – Utopia postponed for those who had a vision of communal planning) through leafy affluent suburbs, to stuccoed commutersville, tenement land and industrial wilderness: all in the space of half an hour.

During the 1989 Glasgow Central by-election I spent three weeks working from a set of rooms just south of the Clyde, in a constituency that was so sprawling, so carved out of the different parts of the city that it was more than possible to get completely and utterly lost, and find oneself on the back of a loudspeaker truck declaiming the candidate's virtues to people who would never have a chance to vote for him. But the rooms were fantastic. They were what remained of an old railway station, massive down below with a variety of smaller meeting and working rooms above. And behind barred-up doors (one of which was still able to be opened) there were old platforms and the artefacts of another age.

They were redolent of another Glasgow – not the down-at-heel city which had turned this public building into a carpet and second-hand furniture shop, but the city in which the smoke of steam trains mixed with the hooting of steamers and the crash of machinery, and in which fortunes were made whilst industrial militancy took root. That contrast in Glasgow is a heady one. The tobacco merchants of the 18th century were replaced by the industrialists of the 19th – James Watt with his vision of the steam condenser which came to him during a walk on Glasgow Green in May 1765, was the begetter of Glasgow's industry, surrounded as it was by coal and iron ore and water. People flocked to Glasgow, through poverty or ambition. The 'dear green place' with the fish and the bell and bird in the tree and St Mungo by the burn was replaced by the 'city of dreadful night' (both of these images conjured up by Glaswegians) and in time by a growing awareness that the gap between rich and poor, between the have and have-nots should not be tolerated.

This book is not the place for a history of Red Clydeside, but the image of the red flag being raised in George Square is one of my favourites. The men who set off from Central Station to get rights for Scottish workers and a decent standard of living were real heroes, the articulators of a Scottish sense of justice that gave birth not just to the first Labour government, but also to a huge improvement in social conditions and in the ambition and expectation of those who, until then, had only the Glasgow Fair and a trip 'doon the watter' to look forward to. Their successors in today's Labour party should hang their heads in shame when they consider the legacy they have squandered. Particularly the legacy of ambition.

I joined the Labour Party at university largely because of that legacy of ambition. Glasgow had proved that those in poverty need not despair but could organise, educate and inform their fellow citizens, and could fall heir – by the ballot box – to the right to build a society that was better than what had gone before. And they could do more: they could reconcile the Protestant and Catholic traditions and engage them both in a search for decency and humanity. One of the great achievements of Labour in West Central Scotland before and after the First World War was to blend Catholic and Protestant into a single political force – without denying the rights of either to wear their badges of identity. And if the unleashed force of religious bigotry disfigured Glasgow at times, it was this political force that bound it up and kept the nightmare of sectarian warfare at bay.

Labour created a sense of belonging – of shared civic pride which could take in the merchants' splendour of the Trades' House and the City Chambers along with the vast housing estates of the northern part of the city, and make a complete and unified city of these seeming opposites. And it did so again and again, so that the very tradition of the city was changed, solidified into a constant campaign for decency for ordinary folk. Being a human structure, of course, there were human failings in it: a grip on the reins of power which excluded other views: a promotion of their own kin over others of similar talent: and the inevitability that power corrupts, and that absolute power does – eventually – corrupt absolutely.

The first real wobble in the edifice of power came in the 1970s – the dichotomy between Labour and the Tories – between the workers and bosses – was upset by the emergence of the SNP which gained a much larger group of councillors than expected. But they were unprepared for power, näive in their expectations and unsophisticated when it came to dealing with real politicians, embedded in local communities. By the end of the decade Labour was back in untrammelled power, and that is the way it has stayed.

Until now. I have walked along to the City Chambers and am talking to an SNP councillor. He is already hearing murmurs of disquiet from council officials, who are positioning themselves for change: Labour is under siege in the City Chambers, with open warfare between members of the Labour group, and an expectation that they will lose their vast majority come the next round of council elections. It would take a landslide to put them out of office, but they may be weakened to the point of collapse if they lose 20 or more seats. That now looks likely – the most recent Glasgow by-election saw a massive swing away from the 'people's party' towards the SNP.

Why? Corruption, says my councillor friend. But also a complete blindness to the purpose of their election. When you can get into office simply by playing the internal political game then your electors become irrelevant. You don't need to do anything for those you are meant to serve, and indeed you don't even need to speak to them. You just make sure that your political patrons, and those you patronise, know their place and their role, and you keep in with them. Politics becomes a speciality, not a service.

As if on cue we are approached by a wee man in a bunnet. He recognises the councillor and wants advice on repairs to his house. He doesn't live in my friend's ward, but he says he has phoned and written and called on his councillor a dozen times, with nothing to show for it. 'Time they were oot on their arses,' he says with a flick of his hand towards the City Chambers behind us. 'They' doesn't need to be defined.

Later I sit down and talk to a Labour councillor – also a friend. He is deeply depressed by what is happening in his party, not least because he is assiduous in his work for his ward, and carries a responsibility within the council that leaves him worn out every day. Like many of his colleagues he has an active social conscience, a radical approach to the problems of his city and a keen desire to see change. He talks of housing conditions in parts of Glasgow that are disgusting and of the shame that the city should feel at its failure to overcome the new problems of social exclusion, drug dealing, unemployment and helplessness. 'It's an impossible task,' he says. 'Glasgow doesn't have the tax base to allow us to raise the money we need to address the problems. It's a city for day visitors now – commuters who use services but contribute nothing. If we could set our own business rate, however, we would scare off too many small businesses and find ourselves again in the eye of the political storm. Government tells us to do more and more with less and less, and the weariness of those who care is weighing us down – we just can't do any more.'

Added to that the internal machinations of the Labour group leave him almost physically sick. 'I've tried not to take sides, just to get on and do the job for which I am elected. But its not possible – if you aren't for someone, you're against them. And if you speak up for the city and its problems, New Labour regards you as a troublemaker.'

He regards losing his seat with equanimity. He thinks the SNP will take it, and wishes the party well of it. 'They can't do any more than we have,' he says. 'They are attractive now because they haven't failed yet. But what Glasgow needs is not a political revolution, but a financial one – a system of local government working hand in hand with national government to put the city back on its feet. Soon there will be two cities – the shopping city, and the living city. Most of the living city is becoming like Beirut!'

Twenty years ago Robert Grieve said that Scotland would only flourish if it solved two problems – Glasgow and the Highlands. Glasgow because of decline, and the Highlands because of depopulation. The Highlands may be in sight of a solution but Glasgow does not appear to have even framed the question yet. But perhaps these views are too pessimistic. The West End flourishes, with the university and the BBC adding their patina of academic and artistic excitement. Every gap site in every suburb appears to have new housing growing up, all for sale and all being sold. In the better council schemes the tell-tale individualistic front doors speak of owner occupation and even in some of the worst areas imaginative restoration has turned the dull rows of council houses into colourful terraces with roof ornaments. Most encouragingly of all, they do not seem to be likely to fall down in the near future.

But go further out, and a sense of desolation is in the air. In Garnethill, in parts of Easterhouse, and in a dozen other places, pull over and stop the car (if you dare) and walk into the closes smelling of urine and rubbish, cluttered with dirt and debris. The walls are decorated with spray-paint graffiti and it is not uncommon to have to step over a comatose body, with or without a needle by its side.

Glasgow has more municipal housing than any other city in Scotland – indeed as a proportion of the housing stock, it is one of the largest totals in Europe. It is inevitable therefore that some of it is decaying and dilapidated, and that some of it will house those who are on the slippery slope down into despond. But what is surprising and alarming is that such decline seems to spread out like a virus, embracing people who want and deserve better and yet who are strangled by it simply because nobody can arrest its progress.

Muir, by his own admission, painted 'a dark picture of Industrialism...in the hope that the evils of present-day Industrialism may be realised and the necessity for taking it in hand brought home as vividly as possible to the reader.' He contrasted the slum life of some of Glasgow's inhabitants with what he called a 'traditional mode of existence' in his beloved Orkney, whilst accepting that Orkney couldn't provide the pattern for the whole country because it had exceptional advantages. We all have the tendency to take the same route when looking at the world. We contrast what we observe with what we find pleasant and acceptable, but sometimes without

Muir's perception that such contrasts are naturally biased towards what we prefer already.

Thus my horror and revulsion at what I saw in the peripheral housing estates in Glasgow arises because of the contrast with the places where I have lived my life – with the place I sit writing this, looking from my desk across my garden to Loch Riddon and the Argyllshire hills. I try and imagine what is like to walk through – to have to walk through – these stinking closes every day, to and from work or shopping or visiting, and feel a shudder of fear.

Yet that is what people have to do. I meet a woman in the close who immediately (it is not difficult) susses me as someone here to write about it, or report it. She takes me into her house, makes me a cup of tea, and talks about how the area has changed. How she came here with her family from the Gorbals, from a flat that was condemned and how she thought it was the best thing she had ever done. 'Now look at it', she says. 'Junkies and kids buying and selling drugs, and rubbish and noise at all hours.'

All she wants is peace and neighbours she can get on with, and perhaps a wee bit of grass outside her house, not the muddy wasteland that lies outwith her door. She blames everyone and no one. The council, the government, people in general, parents who don't care, drink, the television – she blames the 20th century and the way the world is. She has every right to feel this way, but I know (as I know that deep down she does too) that all those who seek to run that same world would do anything to change this place, if they could.

Why can't they?

Money, say some – there isn't the money. Others give the Protestant work ethic solution – just work and all will be fine, and you can afford to better yourself. But try and get a job and keep a job if you live here, and your life is surrounded by failure. Doesn't failure seep into the soul like nerve gas, and numb the ability to compete and rise up? Others still will talk about self-confidence and self-belief. But they are commodities that are not apparent here, except in the most exceptional people. Those exceptional people – or those driven so far by their experiences that they must turn and fight – form community groups and work to make a difference. Sometimes they win for a while and move the problem on to another street and another scheme.

What society is it that is so lacking in perception that it cannot see that the root of despair lies in despair itself: that 'social exclusion' means just that, and that society must change to be inclusive and give hope? That talking about work where there is none is a form of exclusion, and that therefore the first step is to provide decent support structures: benefit that allows people to rise above the poverty line, education and training that doesn't make people poorer while they take part: help for those who are vulnerable that doesn't carry with it the stigma of shame that causes resentment and division.

I am almost ashamed to ask about the Scottish parliament as I have my cup of tea. She is for it, wants to see it happen, wants it to realise that the real Scotland has places like this still in it. And wants those in it to think about, and act on, the root causes of her predicament: the causes of poverty.

Would it be too much to hope that such a crusade could unite all the political parties again – that we could decide that eliminating poverty was the most important task for our new democracy and that the real monument to Scottish progress would be this community back on its feet, with drug abuse and prostitution and despair slowly eradicated? Slowly because it will take time – but that journey of a thousand actions and reactions has to start with the single step of realisation: realisation that as long as one housing estate in our largest city is 'like Beirut' then we have failed as a society, and will go on failing.

Driving away (I chide myself for checking that all the wheels are still on) I wonder what Maxton or Wheatley would have thought if they could have seen that after so many years of Labour control, their city still had places of such shame. It would have redoubled their efforts to change their country for good. Those efforts are still needed – their sense of injustice and passion for their fellow man and woman is still much required.

'For one of the distinguishing marks of Industrialism', Muir wrote in 1935, 'is the permanent contrast between the people who live amidst it, if they are sensitive in any degree or even wish to exist in decency, and all their surroundings. As these people cease to feel the painfulness of this contrast – and they are bound to do so – they inevitably become insensitive; and I think one may assert without being unfair that the middle- and upper-classes of towns like Glasgow, where dirt and squalor are an inseparable and normal part of one's life, even if one has a bath where one can wash them off, or a commodious house where one can forget them, have a sort of comfortable insensitiveness which cannot be found in any other class or in any other place.'

As a nation we have become 'comfortably insensitive' to the continued existence of poverty in our land. It is no longer a problem just for the middle and upper classes of Glasgow – it is a problem for all of us. We must allow ourselves to become coarsely sensitive again so that we can feel the need for change.

There is, however, a huge contrast between Muir's Glasgow of the mid-1930s and today. Or rather a series of huge contrasts. Outwith the peripheral schemes and some of the older areas there is an air of prosperity: Glasgow's self-confidence returned with the late 80s and 90s and the 'Glasgow's Miles Better' campaign, while regarded as a cynical marketing gimmick by some, was inspired and did touch a nerve. The factories belching soot and smoke are largely gone – Clean Air Acts working hand in glove with economic recessions have taken care of that; and although a large part of Victorian Glasgow was destroyed by the builders of the M8 (to the great regret of John Betjeman, who regarded such change as unforgivable vandalism), the remaining buildings of commerce and civic pride have been cleaned and restored. Laid out on a grid system (which was copied by those who built modern Chicago), its centre is logical and accessible, blending theatres and cinemas with shopping and eating – juxtaposing the Scottish Academy of Music and Dramatic Art with the Theatre Royal (for Opera), Scottish Television, the Glasgow Film Theatre, a commercial cinema complex, the Art Club, the School or Art, the College of Piping and numerous restaurants within a couple of blocks.

Unemployment is still a scourge, but not nearly as much as in the 1930s and although the great ships are no longer built within site of the city centre, there are still shipyards around and some heavy industry. But the once crowded river carries little commercial traffic and one of the most frequent sights is that of the last sea-going paddle steamer, *Waverley*, or the sludge boat with its burden of sewage as it heads out to sea every day (and which has on board, more often than not, parties of old-age pensioners enjoying a day out among the sea breezes, oblivious to the humming cargo down below).

Glasgow feels like a place at work, however. Even in the shadow of the new 'armadillo', the extension to the Scottish Exhibition Centre at Finnieston by the Clyde (opposite the derelict site of the National Garden Festival of 1988, which should have been allowed to go on flourishing but which has only been developed extremely slowly), there is a bustle most days in the Moat House Hotel, one of the new fashionable hotels where increasingly Glasgow meets to do business or socialise. The popular heroes – footballers from Rangers or Celtic – are lounging around in the dining-room, rubbing shoulders with politicians holding press conferences or visiting businessmen trying to tie up deals. In the conference rooms sales directors instruct their staff in the quasi-religious beliefs they must espouse and evangelise.

Yet at the top of the stairs I stop astonished by a model of the Glasgow docks at the turn of the century. Occupying this very site they were packed with cargo ships from every corner of the world. The grey bustle of the scene, surrounded by tenements packed with people whose whole livelihood depended upon the river and the jobs it provided in ship building, ship loading, ship unloading, navigation, the transport of passengers and livestock, is awesome; the more so because none of it exists any longer – nothing but the towering bulk of the Finnieston Crane nearby, now preserved as a monument to the city's industrial past.

The reputation of Glasgow as the workshop of the world has drawn waves of immigrants over the past hundred years. Glasgow is, in part, an Irish city – with Irish language classes still held for the small number of families who retain close links with their native land. Glasgow even had a branch of the political party Fianna Fail as recently as the 1980s. Gaels have been a constant feature of the city for over a hundred years, sheltering under the Heilanman's Umbrella, working their way up in nursing, teaching and in most other occupations and giving birth to children who spent their holidays in Lewis, or Uist or Barra or Skye but who were Glaswegians more and more.

Glasgow is also in places an Asian city now, with over 30,000 Asians living mostly on the South Side and in the West End. The vast majority of these people come from Pakistan and Bangladesh and are Moslem – Glasgow has several mosques in addition to the grand new Central Mosque, sitting exotically beside the river and the Sheriff Court. This community is almost a case study of Glasgow as a political city. The prosperous – those who moved from shops to restaurants to property – joined the Tory party and were token guests at dinners and events. Many others joined Labour, and in time some became councillors and one has even become an MP – although an MP in name only as he awaits his assize. No matter the final verdict the publicity has already tarnished the bright hope created by the election of the first Muslim to Westminster.

Now it is the SNP that is attracting the attention of the community. As with all shifts of opinion, it started with one man – Bashir Ahmed, who came to Scotland over 30 years ago and started work as a bus conductor, graduating to driver status, then running a shop, and then a restaurant. His influence was the man from whom he bought his insurance, the former SNP councillor David Smart, who by the usual Scottish small-town coincidence had been the SNP group leader in Clydesdale when I was the parliamentary candidate.

Bashir is a man of tremendous dignity and integrity – a devout Moslem who believes in the goodness of mankind and whose positive vision of racial harmony was boosted in his first hour in Scotland, when the driver of the bus that picked him up at the airport insisted in taking him to the very door of the house whose address he had been given, scribbled on a piece of paper.

It was Bashir who heard Alex Salmond speak at a dinner of the Pakistan Welfare Association, and Bashir who followed it up by inviting Alex to meet and discuss the Asian community and its political needs. It was Bashir who decided to set up Scots Asians for Independence – to bring the Asian community into contact with the SNP and to dispel the smears about the party which Labour was constantly spreading. And it was Bashir who, convinced that independence was the right goal for the country he now called home, set about recruiting members of the community to join the party.

I have now spoken at, or attended, numerous dinners, house meetings and events organised by Scots Asians. Each time it is like entering politics afresh – arguing from first principles about justice, equality and prosperity; learning about traditions which are dear to the community and blending them with my own views on life; listening to real stories about racial prejudice, harassment and discrimination and the way in which individuals have coped with such experiences. I have watched as the organisation grew and as more and more joined the SNP – always after much reflection and discussion and have helped to train those who wanted to participate in the party at every level and encouraged them when disappointment was the result of their first try.

But most of all, I marvel at a community, so far from its roots, struggling to maintain its core values and beliefs while also endeavouring to be part of the society it has joined: to affirm its badges of identity while willingly taking on new badges and their responsibilities. Perhaps it is true that those who know only Scotland, cannot really know Scotland at all. For in the Glasgow Muslim community there is a stronger affection for, and devotion to, the future of our country than you would find at many a Burns supper. For so many Scots the future of Scotland is a matter almost of indifference – or at least that was the case until the referendum last year, when Scotland seemed to wake from its slumber and start to address its future.

In the Scots Asian community the task of making a new Scotland is a living challenge. Certainly it affords the opportunity to bring to that new Scotland some of their concerns and loyalties – but it also affords the opportunity for them to be once and for all an equal part of the country in which they have chosen to live. There is also a warmth in the community that speaks of something we have lost. A warmth bred from being strangers in a strange land, no doubt, of the necessity to group together, but also a warmth of shared belief and of a purposeful approach to the future.

Yet that purposeful approach is not uncritical – nor should it be. One of the members – an accountant, and an Urdu poet – said at a dinner I attended recently that 'Labour and Tory have promised this community much when seeking our votes, but when in power have given us little. Our challenge to you is to do better – and we are willing to work with you to that end. The result we wait to see.' They have been disappointed by politics, as so many in Scotland have. Out of their disappointment – out of their thirst for real change – has come a support for a different way for Scotland. We are all, even those of us at the heart of it, waiting to see the result – waiting to be measured against the challenge of making this a country fit for all its people.

Scots Asians has also given to those who are involved a sense of belonging. It is good to walk down a street in Pollokshaws and be greeted by people one would never normally have met – to go into their houses and see that they are, in their own individual ways, striving to improve their lives and those of their friends and neighbours. They are personally affronted by the poverty and loss of some who live in their city and actively seek ways in which society can change to help the helpless and honour those who have been dishonoured by their circumstances. And they are revolted by the corruption and lack of principle that has passed for civic politics in Glasgow for too long, and which has touched their community.

I am conscious that in what I have written I have found Glasgow to be – as Muir did – a city of contrasts, yet so big that the contrasts themselves contain contradictions. It is almost baffling to start defining the city, let alone complete the analysis.

But unlike Muir I have an affection for the city: for the crass vulgarity of the 'Barras' and the sales patter of the stall holders, sucking in money by their beguiling, eccentric, fulsome charm: for the calm of the Botanic Gardens and the Kibble Palace: for the functional elegance of the School of Art and for Charles Rennie MacIntosh who, no matter how abused his reputation has been by popular taste in recent years, remains a defining Scottish voice in stone and wood on a truly international scale.

But when I return to my purpose for this journey – my purpose in finding out what it is that Scotland is 'in waiting' for – Glasgow provides both easy answers and some difficult evasions. Easy answers because Glasgow has more than its fair share of problems. It needs better local government, more resources to spend on its services, a programme to eradicate poverty, an active race relations policy and an emphasis on the things it excels at – the media, industry and commerce, and tourism. And difficult evasions because Glasgow, the largest of Scotland's cities (though well down on the million souls that Muir observed), is too diverse to admit to simple solutions. It evades definition, and its problems therefore need more than simple knee-jerk reactions. In a sense the new Glasgow – the Glasgow that was a European City of Culture, which hosted a Garden Festival and which is still developing its Merchant City

– is already showing what self-confidence can do, is already in advance of what a parliament might bring. And the old Glasgow of dreadful nights and smoky railway stations is dead and buried. It is the in-between Glasgow that is so complex – the city that allows its dreadful schemes to fall into the hands of drug dealers and become, as the councillor said, 'like Beirut' – the Glasgow which often seems to be intractable, to be beyond mere political intervention and political solution. The Glasgow which could either disappear itself, with the last needle in the last vein, and the last Transit van taking the last citizen to a better home, or could spread and poison all that is being achieved.

I have a feeling that the answer lies in Glasgow itself, not in the parliament per se. And by that I mean that Glasgow has to solve its problems itself – has to re-invent itself by paying attention to what is wrong and using the resilience and the determination of its people to step forward. Glasgow in the new parliament needs strong Glasgow voices. It needs people who are part of their communities and listening to them, people who will agitate for and get the resources they need – but who will also mobilise the inherent strength of Glasgow to tackle poverty, social exclusion and despair.

200,000 Glaswegians fought in the First World War, as the Cenotaph in George Square records. They went to make a land fit for heroes to live in, and then came back and had to fight all over again in order to send to Westminster their authentic, battling voices. Glasgow, to a great degree, led Scotland and Britain in the fight for social justice. The fact that it is not yet achieved in their back yard simply means that the fight is not yet over. It is Glasgow voices that will be needed to carry it on.

Muir finished his visit to the city with these words: 'The fundamental realities of Glasgow are economic. How is this collapsing city to be put on its feet again?' Perhaps in the same way as it happened after Muir; by the efforts of Glasgow's representatives themselves, and by their vision and determination. Economic problems there are – but now also are the problems of psyche and self-confidence that lack of economic success provokes.

Robert Grieve was right. Let's solve the problem of Glasgow so that we can have the land that is good enough for all of us. That solution lies in Glasgow's own hands.

Chapter Seven
Stirling and Perth

'The surroundings of Glasgow are beautiful, especially to the North where the Highlands begin', wrote Muir, having shaken the grimy dust of the city off his feet. But he was not being entirely accurate, geographically speaking. Heading north-west the flood plain of the Clyde gives way to Loch Lomond and then the Highlands – within an hour of leaving Glasgow city centre by car you can be entering Crianlarich and amongst real mountains, but go to the north-east – taking the road to Stirling – and you are still firmly in Central Scotland.

Muir dallied when leaving Glasgow – animadverting on the Clyde coast resorts and anguishing about his experiences in Greenock, before turning into Lanarkshire. Only then did he seek the fresh air of the road northwards, passing 'a cloud of dense darkness where Falkirk lay round its furnaces', before coming to Stirling. Today the route from Glasgow is more direct. Yet another motorway goes from the centre of the city out almost to Cumbernauld – within a year or two it is planned to pass that new town and link up with the Stirling road, at the point at which you can now cross the little waist of Scotland and take the Kincardine Bridge to Fife and the east.

This is one of the busiest roads in Scotland, with the names of the Castlecary Arches or the roundabout at

Mollinsburn near Cumbernauld being daily litanies in the traffic reports. I have often spent half or three quarters of an hour here trapped in a traffic jam, trying just to get out of Glasgow and into Central Scotland. But modern traffic planners are moving against new roads and if this link is not improved or replaced then the only solution will be to find a way – some way – of cutting down the traffic that uses it.

There are usually hitch-hikers at some stage on the road, and although I stopped giving lifts when I left the Western Isles 15 years ago, today I pick one up as I leave a filling station on the road, to talk to him about why he is travelling and where he is going. Bob is in his early twenties, and hitching to see his girlfriend in Stirling. He has just left university, and is looking for a job – though with a general arts degree he doesn't really know what he can do – or what he wants to do.

He hitches because it is free – but he admits that if he had the money for the train fare from Glasgow he would probably still hitch. 'You meet people', he says, 'and you don't have to stand all the way, or be pushed about by drunks going to Aberdeen.' He tells me of a journey he took recently from Dundee to Edinburgh on the train – coming back from a job interview. The train was half an hour late, and when it arrived it was crowded.

'I got a place in the corridor, but I was next to three roughnecks on their way back to Tyneside after a month on the rigs. They had been drinking all day, and one kept leaning out the window to be sick, and then taking another can of export and downing it virtually in one. I though he would die, but he just seemed to be topping himself up, and then getting rid of the surplus.

'There was a wee old woman who had to stand too. She got fed up with the language and the drinking and tried to get the guard to do something. He sort of circled the three lads for a while, but didn't say anything. When I got off at Edinburgh so did the old woman – but she was really wanting to go on to Newcastle. The last I saw of her she was trying to complain to someone but behind her the train was pulling out again, and there was a very obvious 'V' sign coming from her carriage door. And a sudden ejection of something else!'

Bob is ambiguous about politics – almost unconcerned. But he has voted SNP and might do again. His ideal parliament is one that would get jobs for graduates, although his vagueness about exactly which jobs seems to make this a difficult requirement to fulfil. He doesn't like the idea of politicians being paid. 'Why can't we just have people who do it, and that's it', he says disarmingly, but when I mention the state of my personal finances, my mortgage and my dogs and cats to feed, he swings round to the notion that payment is probably a reasonable enough idea after all.

His apparent lack of engagement in the political process should be worrying – but as it is something I seem to find in everyone I meet who is under 30 years of age (except the political groupies – those who want a career in politics and who are gravitating naturally towards the SNP these days). I suspect it is just a weariness about the log-jam of Scotland's affairs: he seems to have already accepted that independence is long overdue, but all he is concerned about is that he doesn't have to pay for it. A type of political hitch-hiking then, I suggest to him, and he has the good grace to smile.

Today the road isn't too busy and we are soon at the Stirling turn-off. He gets out at the motorway services – his girlfriend works there – and thanks me for the lift. As he walks away a drunk staggers to the kerbside, lager can in hand, trying to thumb a lift. I remember Bob's ScotRail journey from hell and drive off fast.

For most of the people outside the central belt and the other major Scottish cities such as Aberdeen and Dundee, a car is not a luxury, but a necessity. In fact, if you don't live within a city or a large town, public transport is either not available, or not reliable and convenient. Muir's Scotland was different. Trains went from every hole in the hedge and buses joined every village to their neighbouring town. The car partly killed that type of infrastructure, but it was also killed by a lack of foresight from local government allied to a lack of investment in basic public transport services for which we are still paying the price.

A sensible public transport system would create holding areas for cars outside each major city, with first-class, frequent public transport from these places into every part of each city. And it would make such public transport either free or extremely cheap and accessible every hour of the day and night. The only solution which we are offered at the moment seems to be to make the use of the motor car (irrespective of where the driver lives) an increasing financial burden while failing to offer any improvement for the public element. Lots of sticks, but precious few carrots.

In any case for all of rural Scotland there is likely to be no transport alternative to the car. If I, living in Argyll, want to travel by bus or train to Edinburgh, I might as well don my Marco Polo gear, wave my wife and son good-bye, and set out on the great journey. I would first of all have to walk down a 500-yard track (my choice, I admit, and I'm prepared to fully accept my responsibility for stage one), then I'd take a bus (one every two hours) to Dunoon, which would take almost an hour. The boat trip across would be another half-hour, and then a train to Glasgow would take 40 minutes. I would change stations (15 minutes) and take an hour-long train journey to Edinburgh, with a further 15-minute walk to my office. Total time: almost four hours – or more if I am staggering under the weight of my laptop and my overnight bag. But more pertinently, the cost is also prohibitive – about £25 all in compared to the ferry fare of about £5.00 if you buy the tickets in bulk, and the £10 worth of diesel I would need (all right, all right, I know that I also have to cost in car depreciation, the running costs, etc, etc...but it is not only cheaper, it *seems* cheaper).

Some of my neighbours would have an even more difficult time. Sandy MacQueen, who lives across the loch would be best to take his boat over to the Island of Bute (an hour and a half to Rothesay) and catch a ferry to the mainland from there. If not he would have to walk a three-mile track and get one of the increasingly rare buses – the best would be the subsidised Post Bus – to start his trip to Dunoon.

Somehow we're going to have to live with the car in rural Scotland (and perhaps be a bit more fair on petrol and ferry prices), whilst making it easy in the towns and cities to use what is laid on for us. Best to lay it on first, and make it attractive, than try and force a change. Motorway tolls and punitive car tax increases are not the first steps, even with some vague commitment to hypothecation of the proceeds. Governments have a tendency to forget such promises once the money starts rolling in.

There is virtually no public transport to the field of Bannockburn, which I pass on my way into Stirling. But the sight of it always gives me sore feet, as I have marched to it from the centre of Stirling year in and year out on the third Saturday in June. The SNP's Bannockburn Rally has been a fixed point in the nationalist calendar for many years. In the 60s and 70s there were usually two or three thousand marchers, complete with pipe bands and regalia.

Today the numbers are down to two or three hundred at each event – not a sign of lessening of interest in nationalism, but more a sign that such interest need not be expressed by an annual airing of the Saltire. Younger party members are keener to campaign than to march (it used to be the other way round at university) and the time is right for a different type of event to mark the anniversary of the battle – a festival or a fair perhaps?

Muir 'remembered' about Bannockburn when leaving Stirling by way of the Wallace Monument on the other side of the town. At that time there was a dispute about the real site of the battle, and who should preserve the field. The National Trust won, and it is now a typical NT property – superficially attractive, but with a host of regulations about its use and a seemingly paranoiac fear pervades the place preventing anyone from actually being passionate about it.

Unlike Culloden, Bannockburn has little atmosphere left. There is nothing brooding about the site – it is wide and open, and crossed by the M90 – and only at the modern-day statue of Bruce does one get any impression of the magnitude of what was won here: nothing less than Scotland's freedom and an independent state that lasted for almost four hundred years thereafter.

I park the Land-Rover and walk out onto the field. At the borestone I meet an elderly American couple, trying to make sense of the place. Al and Jean are from New York, and she claims Scottish ancestry. We talk about Scotland and its past and I describe the events leading up to 1314. They, however, are more interested in how I know about this – we get on to politics and they tell me they have come to Scotland this year, for their first visit, because they had read about the referendum and about how we are going to be independent.

I try to explain to them that we aren't quite independent yet but the concept is difficult for them. 'You mean', says Al, 'that you are still going to be giving your oil away? And that you can't raise taxes? Are you nuts, or something?'

They have the idea, and I agree that we may be nuts, but we are working on a cure. Unusually it is Jean that is the redneck of the pair – in looking at the panorama around us I mention Dunblane and the gun ban, and she reacts almost violently. 'Guns ain't the problem', she spits, 'it's the people with the guns'. She warms to the subject, much to Al's embarrassment. 'If those teachers had had guns, they would have blown that guy away,' she asserts, beginning to poke me in the chest. 'If those policemen had had guns, they would have sorted that guy out before he did what he did...[poke, poke]...if the parents of the kids he had tried it on with before...[she is well informed – there must be a National Rifle Association briefing sheet on this in America]...had had guns, they would have dealt with him.'

For once in my life I am beginning to wish I had a gun. But I can't stop her, or change her mind. Of all the gulfs that separate us from our cousins across the pond, gun laws are the most intractable. I once had to appear on NBC talking about the SNP proposals for a ban on all handguns, and it was as if I had told the French that total abstinence (and a prohibition on cheese and Gauloise) was the only way forward. Incredulity was the kindest part of it.

The fusillade subsides, and I give them a lift into Stirling, as they have taken a taxi out. They are going on to Inverness, and then back to Glasgow. They too are using the trains, but they seem enchanted by them. Enchanted, that is, by everything but the lack of seats and the speed. 'Why don't you guys go a bit a faster, and have enough places for everyone?' asks Al. I say I don't know as I have probably done enough to confuse them for one day. A dissertation on the troubles brought on by privatisation would have been an explanation too far.

Muir found Stirling 'bright, solid and stylish' but as usual, when standing looking at the 'impressive prospect' that can be seen from the castle he could not help remarking on the old tenements in the town which had, like those 'in almost all Scottish historical cities…largely degenerated into slums'. Now the slums have become fashionable homes and restaurants – even fashionable hotels – and the one-way traffic system, with its chicanes and bumps for 'calming' traffic makes the whole area quieter though I suspect much less authentic.

I can never visit Stirling Castle without recalling the final moments of *Tunes of Glory*, the film of the Kennaway novel, and the snow drifting into the ramparts as the pipes die away. Even at one of the final Runrig concerts held here on a summer evening in 1997 I felt cold, but also moved. Or rather I did once I had persuaded a large German fan to take down his huge banner (*The Black Forest says Hullo to Runrig – You are the Greatest*) which was blocking the view of the stage for about 20 percent of the audience.

Stirling lies at the heart of Scotland – but just as the heart, whilst vital, is not the most attractive of organs, Stirling itself always seems one of the less desirable of Scottish towns. Rather than concentrating on the town's assets, one is always mindful of what one can see from it and where it lies – to the east the flat lands of the Forth, and the refinery stacks of

Grangemouth, as well as a smudge on the landscape of the Hillfoots villages; to the west beyond the carse the start of the conglomeration that has Glasgow in its midst; to the south a nondescript landscape edging into industrialisation. Only to the north do the hills of the Highlands offer the prospect of real, fresh, rural Scotland.

I am going north, and set out again past Stirling Bridge and the university, which is really in Bridge of Allan, the neighbouring town. Soon I am skirting Dunblane, driving on the bypass that sweeps in a lazy half-circle round that unhappy little town. For years Dunblane was simply a name on the road – the old A9 passed through it, and in the summer it was not uncommon to be stuck for 20 minutes in the traffic queue that built up on either side of the roundabout above the old town centre. Then the new road was built, and only rarely did I find myself driving down to the Cathedral and the attractive main street, usually because I needed a paper, or a bottle of wine to take home. Dunblane was, and is, a commuter town with a good rail service, to Glasgow in particular. A number of acquaintances at the BBC lived there, travelling in each day. It was one of many such towns, no more remarkable than any other.

Now its name is unforgettable. I suspect for many Scots the day of the tragedy will become like the day of Kennedy's assassination for Americans. One will remember where one was when the news came through, and how one hovered around the television trying to make sense of the unfolding story. I was showing the SNP's bank manager round the office for the first time, when I glanced at the Teletext that is always on in the press office. 'Ten Children Dead'. I went over and checked the story – by the time I had refreshed the screen it was up to 'Eleven Children'. And it went on rising.

For the rest of the day there was a constant stream of phone calls – enquiries about what we were saying, which seemed irrelevant, and friends who just wanted to talk. Margaret Ewing went to Dunblane (she used to live there) and was shattered by the experience – seeing at first hand not only the grief but also meeting those who were trying to cope with it, and seeing the enormity of what they had witnessed. Hardened journalists rang to debate in private the ethics of dealing with the story, and how they didn't want to intrude but had to report it. My wife and I talked about how it could happen anywhere, even in her little school of 20 pupils, which – like all schools – had no security and an open door.

The day after I had the worst migraine of my life: physically sick perhaps with the difficulty of comprehending the sheer evil of the event. 'Evil' is a word I eschew, preferring to account for wrong by the damage that individuals suffer in their lives, and hoping for reformation rather than bringing into play arbitrary judgement. But evil is the only word for it. A blackness within an individual so great – perhaps a pain so great – that it turned into a rain of death upon those who had no blame, and who turned their faces to their intruder at first in enquiry and welcome and only then in innocent, wounded, uncomprehending terror.

I drive on past the town; now frozen in the echo of the pistol shots that have changed this place forever. It deserves to be left in peace, to bind itself up and to heal itself, supported by our anguished love, but not burdened with our continued, prurient, enquiries.

Between Stirling and Perth the countryside starts to rise up, erecting little hills as homages to the Highlands to come. Off to the right is Sheriffmuir – another Scottish battle scene, though the drive to it does not repay any curiosity: there is nothing there but a few houses, and the pub that used to house Hercules the Bear, whose escape in the Western Isles some years ago caused me not a little worry, as he swam off to freedom from an island that I could see clearly from my bedroom in Benbecula.

I pass Blackford, home to both the sleeping Tullibardine Distillery and the constantly operational Highland Spring water plant, the former now under the ownership of Jim Beam Brands and the latter owned by Arabs and aggressively marketed throughout the world. Muir would have been amazed that the same Scottish water upon which the whisky industry depends has become an important asset in its own right, and will be more important still in the next century, when water becomes a scarce resource. In fact Muir would probably be amazed by many of the ways in which Scots now earn their living – bottling water, assembling with infinite care small slivers of silicon that could contain all his books hundreds of times over; erecting windmills to generate power; selling hamburgers to car drivers at small glass side windows – even running the day to day affairs of political parties.

All these can certainly be fitted into the endless interplay of 'exploiters and exploited' that Muir observed with disgust (and which, in its 1934 form he believed had led to the decline of Scotland and its identity), but somehow that definition does not quite fit our country today. The market economy can still be savage and unrestrained – the legions of the unemployed that still exist will testify to that – but equally it can be inventive, creative and positive: it can re-invent itself in a million ways, and bring a million new benefits to society.

'The market has no morality' was a Michael Heseltine boast, intended to signify the need for governments to keep out of freebooting capitalism. But the market is operated by human beings, who do have moral choices. They do not have to bow to every market trend or force, or make profit the only criteria by which they will be judged. They can make moral choices about the level of profit, about the need to invest in human beings as well as plant and machinery, and then can seek to ameliorate any negative effects of the market on employees and communities.

They can, in short, bring morality into the market place as a factor – and bring in human decency and human responsibility too, the responsibility of one person to another; the duty of care. The ludicrous construct of Blair's 'third way' would make a little (though not much) sense if this is what it meant – if it meant listening to people and their concerns, and accepting the legitimate fears and concerns of trade unions and their members. But this is not a 'third way' at all – it is a modern version of European Social Democracy, in which individuals have rights and exercise those in tandem with their duties as members of society: and in which society too can exercise care and responsibility.

A true socialism – Muir's socialism – is possibly the ideal way to regulate human life. But it is also impossible to achieve, at least at this moment in time. The best we can do is to accept and embrace the benefits of capitalism and find ways of regulating and reforming its worst aspects. Ways that can provide a shield for the failures of the market, but still enjoy its successes, and use them to invest in our future.

I am thinking about social theory when I find myself speeding past the Gleneagles Hotel, a temple of capitalist success which has wisely invested in a splendid new golf course that edges the road. I am glad that such excesses exist – which probably condemns me to the purists as the worst sort of romantic hedonist. But inventing a new golf course is a noble activity: a blending of ingenuity and culture to create something that will test and reward in unequal measure. From there I skirt the long village of Auchterarder and start the hill climb to Perth. Off to my left is the wonderfully named Findo Gask, the sign to which used to beckon me from the old road every time I came this way. Eventually I went, and drove for miles without finding anything. Does it exist? Is it my Nirvana, I wonder, which I am fated forever to seek? Or is it just yet another superb Scottish placename, the romance of which is far greater than its actuality.

I am very fond of Perth and was even before I spent five weeks here in the run up to the constituency by-election in 1995. It is a pity that Muir devotes only one line to it – 'I stopped in Perth to buy a basket of strawberries and pushed on to a remote part of Angus where I wished to see a married couple, old friends of mine, who were running a farm there' – as to me it is one of the most Scottish of towns, and yet also one of the most modern. Like all Scottish towns it has simply grown – so driving in is a patchwork experience, moving past modern estates to Edwardian villas and on to car showrooms, tyre depots and then into the town centre itself.

Perth sits comfortably on the River Tay, and the best of the centre abuts onto the river itself, with traffic guided over two bridges, which are (unusually) the boundaries of the city. Perth is a city, and calls itself such – with some justification as it is the fastest-growing conurbation in Scotland, and will, in size, overtake Dundee early in the next century. It has already overtaken Dundee in attraction.

There is little in the centre that is really old – or at least looks that way, apart from St John's Kirk, which is the cradle of the Scottish Reformation. The impressive City Chambers look late-18th century, tarted up a bit in the next century, but they sit cheek by jowl with shops and offices, and with a wealth of pubs and restaurants that make the city a good place to spend an evening. Such an integration of civic activity and service is just the right note to strike.

Perth is also rich in hotels, my favourite being the Salutation – though its claim to be the oldest hotel in Scotland is probably bogus. None the less, and despite the ravages of the all-purpose modern hotel interior designer, it has a comfortable and antique feel, with a splendid window in the first floor dining room that gives a view of a single city street that speaks volumes about the place. And it certainly did play host to Charles Edward Stewart during his triumphal sweep down Scotland in 1745 – a sweep that was exceeded in speed only by his retreat the following year!

Modernism has made the main shopping thoroughfare as bland as anywhere else in Scotland – there is even an indoor mall – yet the streets constantly surprise, producing small faded cafés, and strange shops dedicated to odd fashions or pursuits in every nook and cranny. Even the straight and ordered Victorian part of the centre – slightly grim with its severe tenements – has a variety that is hard to find elsewhere.

Perth is also prosperous – an Aga dealership gives testimony to the wealth of the surrounding countryside, as does a Laura Ashley outlet. But its community spirit means that the Perth Theatre lies almost next to that imported centre of home counties good taste, and round the corner one can hire a kilt from an old-fashioned tailor that looks (and is) planted in the last century. Perth City Halls lie at the heart of the city and although they are too small now for the type of political conference that is the norm, there has been an attempt to make them more attractive by sprinkling pavement cafés around. Inside the wood-panelled splendour has been restored and the gold leaf re-gilded: only the massive organ sits mute, waiting for someone knowledgeable enough to make its sound fill the building.

Perhaps I like Perth because I associate it with success: it was here that Alex Salmond become SNP leader in 1990, and at the same time, as his campaign manager, I avoided being defeated for the party office I held. I spent the only real sleepless night of my life before that vote, working out in my head again and again whether we had really done things the right way, and if so was there any possibility of defeat. My head said no, but my usual caution said, 'Of course...anything can happen.' And in 1995 I ran the campaign that won the by-election – again saying to myself for days before that we must win because no one else could, yet constantly questioning whether the right things were taking place, and whether the right campaign was being run. But I also associate Perth with long evenings and pleasant dinners, good company and dry weather and a sense of wellbeing enhanced by the surroundings and the people.

There is no doubt that this eastern part of Scotland (we are only 20 miles or so from the sea, and the river Tay that runs through here will soon be broad enough to require a massive road bridge at Dundee) is drier and the ambient weather better than the west where I live and where I was brought up. That fact seems to be reflected in the bustle and style of the city – less hiding from the rain and the wind, and more openness and casual conversation. Perhaps I am imagining it, but the strong voices of the farmers and their wives greeting each other in the open streets is a sound I don't associate with Oban or Fort William: there the conversation is more intimate, the gatherings more huddled.

Tonight I am having dinner with work colleagues, preparing for a special party conference. Out of the richness of choice we select a Thai restaurant (I have been there before with the BBC) and we have an excellent meal, though the table keeps expanding as more people turn up, and the nervous waiter is beginning to have a breakdown as his work expands also. The talk revolves in small groups, occasionally widening to embrace the whole table, then falling apart again into twos and threes. Inevitably it as about what we share – the minutiae of the moment, of polls and problems, and possibilities ahead. Allison Hunter – with whom I have run six by-elections and innumerable other campaigns – mentions an incident from the last campaign here: within moments we are reminiscing about events and personalities and drawing in an audience of younger party members, now staff, who are sharing the culture and, in the semiotic parlance, 'owning' the incidents.

This is not a unique event: any group of people who work together know the syndrome, and know that it is a fragile covering of common experiences that lies over the vast deep of personal lives, ambitions, histories and futures. We are, in William MacIlvanney's phrase, 'swapping names like conversation', but it is the conversation that unites us, and it is therefore comforting, reassuring and re-enforcing. Eventually we pay, and walk out into an early summer street that is still bright with the reflected light of northern hemisphere evenings. There are shafts of sunlight lying along the road, spilling into the town from the surrounding hills. A couple of us walk to the river, which is rolling and surging towards the sea, but controlled and quiet in this season, glassy on its top in the calm air.

Much later I am ensconced in MP Roseanna Cunningham's office, reacting to a new poll and coming to terms with the fact that to the younger members of our staff the confidence and self-assertion of Scottish voters is not a surprise, but an inevitability. Even if it declines from here on in, even if Scotland draws back for a moment from embracing its future and stepping onto the world stage as itself, it will still only be a temporary setback for them.

They are confident – with the confidence of youth – that the future does belong to them, and that such a future will be better, more open and more generous than the age in which they grew up. For me, that hope is summed up in a place like Perth. An ancient city, it has taken part in many of the major events of our history, yet has gone on growing and developing and being renewed. It took the Union in its stride, and it can take a new future just as well. To the outside it may seem quiet and conservative. But it has a will and a spirit of its own. It wants to be part of the world, and it will make it on its own terms.

The river keeps on running to the sea. The town keeps on growing. And the people keep on living here, welcoming new blood and enlisting them in the quiet, determined, civilised, cause of the city.

Chapter Eight
Aberdeen and Inverness

At last I am out of Central Scotland, or at least would be if I didn't have to go north to Aberdeen. That sentence seems to contain a geographical or directional contradiction. But 'Central Scotland', or 'the Lowlands' with which it is sometimes wrongly conflated, is not just a description of place. It also describes in general terms the divide in Scotland between the high ground and the islands to the north and west – those places above the Highland Boundary Fault that splits our country in two – and the part that lies below it. That part includes most of the east of the country, and it certainly includes Aberdeen.

Muir did not visit Aberdeen – perhaps he saw no need to, because when he wrote in the mid 1930s it was, although the northernmost city of the nation, a comparatively poor and unregarded city, making its living from fishing and not much else. Today, of course, it is the Houston or Dallas of Scotland – our oil capital whose wealth fuelled the engine of Thatcherism and whose promise can still be of importance to us as we approach the 21st century.

As is common in Scotland the development of a place of importance is only followed by the improvement of transport links – there is a period of chaos in between, when the roads are inadequate and the train services non-existent. The main road to Aberdeen is now dual carriageway for all of its length, but that has only happened in the last few years. Up until then one had to cope with endless roadworks and a drive through Stonehaven, a pleasant seaside holiday town which was in danger of being ruined by the thundering of heavy lorries.

The process of making Aberdeen accessible is still not complete, however. Although I am approaching it from the south, I intend to drive on to Inverness, and the A96 is still in places an ordinary road, with endless delays from accidents or just plain pressure of traffic. I put that problem out of my mind, and the fact that I am going to have to make this journey in a single day – not a very sensible decision, as I am to find out.

Perth to Dundee is a commuter route, the road sprinkled with signs alerting the motorist to the presence of police speed checks, or police cameras. The camera signs are confusing – apparently Japanese tourists have sometimes taken them not as warnings, but as invitations to take photographs from a particularly good spot. There are no verges full of snapping orientals as I drive along, but there are police cars tucked into driveways and farm roads: there is a speeding campaign underway.

Dundee is not my favourite Scottish city, but I will admit that, approaching it from the Perth side, it does look inviting: the modern hospital on the side of the hill looks like a shining city (how Reaganesque) and Riverside Drive gives not only a view of the pillars of the old Railway Bridge, but a wide open panorama of the Firth of Tay. I would like to divert today and drive over the road bridge to St Andrews, only a few miles away on the other side of the Tay. Muir went to live in St Andrews but was not happy there.

However it was the scene of a memorable encounter between Muir and MacDiarmid, in the summer of 1936, after *Scott on Scotland* had appeared. George Bruce was visiting his uncle, Francis George Scott who was also spending time in a borrowed house in the town, and arrived to find 'FG' as he was called, furious and gesticulating at the paragraphs in Muir's book that condemned the use of Lallans. Bruce went to visit Muir shortly afterwards 'to have it out with him' but also to warn him that MacDiarmid was likely to be even more incensed. But Muir was quite relaxed about the matter, saying only that 'borderers' (MacDiarmid, of course, being one) were quite likely to overreact.

The overreaction came swiftly – MacDiarmid duly arrived and had a shouting match with Muir (MacDiarmid shouted, Muir kept quite calm) and then stormed out, finishing what had been a productive friendship, and replacing it with a long-standing bitter enmity, at least on MacDiarmid's side. That bad feeling extended to MacDiarmid failing to include Muir in his *Golden Treasury* anthology.

I have only visited St Andrews on a few occasions since I was a child living in Elie but have always been taken by its unique mixture of small town, golfing and tourist mecca and university city. I am told that for students it gets claustropho-bic after a while but somewhere in my imagination its diversity within such a compact space strikes me as the ideal resting place – the place to grow old in, surrounded by learning, by familiarity and by old Scottish pursuits and customs. St Andrews though will have to wait, as I have an appointment to keep in Dundee, and then a long day's drive ahead.

Allan (it is not his real name – he doesn't want that used) has written me a letter asking about the possibility of standing as an SNP candidate for the Scottish Parliament. There have been lots of such letters in the last few months, from those with no previous party affiliation but who are motivated to do something political at last. Most have had a kind but firm reply – a year's party membership is the basic requirement, without which no application can be entertained. If you have that qualification then you can apply, and will be interviewed and put through a training weekend. But – the final clincher – applications closed in April (they had to – the elections are next May).

I have agreed to see Allan because his application was a

little different from the rest. He is in his late forties, a highly successful businessman with a national reputation. I had – when I saw him quoted – always assumed he was a Tory, but he tells me that he has never been a member of a political party, and actually voted Liberal at the last election.

'I spend a lot of time travelling overseas' he says. 'Lately I have been saying to myself – what is different about Scotland, that we can't play to our strengths and put ourselves about in the world? And I can't find any answer, short of the restrictions that are placed on us from a UK government that always speaks for us.'

Allan's political ambitions are vague and ill formed. I have sent him some literature on the party and he finds nothing in it that he can't either accept or at least agree amicably to abide by. But as we talk it becomes obvious that day to day politics aren't for him – he is too used to deciding for himself, rather than collectively. He does, though, want to do something for the new political circumstances we are in.

'I've done very well', he says, 'but know I want to be part of this new politics I hear about. I'm a bit nervous about any party – it seems so often to be ya boo stuff you see reported – but the SNP may have the potential to make something different.'

We talk about involvement in his local area, but he doesn't want that. And we talk about involvement in Business for Scotland – a group of nationalist minded businessmen that has just been formed. Yet he is unsure about that also. We are now clutching at straws – his is a wish to be part of our new country: mine is a desire to have him involved. But how? It is like the parable of the young man who wanted to be a disciple but who would not sell all that he had and give to the poor.

We leave the matter open – he will think about things he can do, and I will come back to him. Dissatisfied, I get into my car for the next part of the road: there are lots of people who want to be involved but who find conventional politics not to their liking, and their own lifestyles too comfortable to change. Perhaps the lack of activism that all political parties bemoan arises from this core problem – the problem that Oscar Wilde summarised when he said that the trouble with socialism is that it takes up too many evenings! Or perhaps no party as yet has found the way to enrol and energise those who would otherwise stay at home.

The SDP briefly succeeded, but wilted in the shadow of one man's ambition. Blair talks a lot of the 'Sedgefield model' – the way in which he claims to have created a dynamic, mass-membership party in his own constituency. But the more one examines it, the less it holds water – it is a glorified social club with powerless members acting merely as political groupies. One or two SNP organisations – in nearby Angus for example – have a strong track record of success built on thriving branches. But even their numbers, while growing, are not at the levels that they were in the 1970s. No party's are, no matter the spin they try to put on them.

Political party mass membership may be something from the past. But harnessing the energy and desire of people to participate in change must remain a political ambition. There has never been a better time, but to do it parties will have to change and become more open and more accountable. The SNP is not full up, as I repeatedly tell branches – but it can look that way, if most local activity is jealously guarded by two or three people.

I navigate my way back to the ring road, aware again that Dundee seems to have too much in all the wrong places – industrial estates sit side by side with rows of 1930's bungalows, and old tenements give way suddenly to modern libraries. Dundee always seems to have been thrown down, scattered along a shore with no organisation and no plan. Even its up-market suburb of Broughty Ferry, with its grid plan by the sea, contains too much variety and none of it neatly ordered.

I am now heading north, through the prosperous lands of Angus and the Mearns. You can travel on the coast road, dipping in and out of Arbroath and Montrose until you rejoin the main thoroughfare at Stonehaven. But it is faster and more direct to cut across country, with the new bypasses skirting Forfar and Laurencekirk, and with only signposts to indicate the attractive villages that lie on every side – Edzell, St Cyrus and the rest.

After an hour I am in Lewis Grassic Gibbon country – the rich farmlands that run from the sea to the foothills of the Grampians. Grassic Gibbon – or James Leslie Mitchell to give him his real name – was a genuine socialist (a Communist Party member at one time) with a devotion to his native soil that was strong and radical. The *Sunset Song* trilogy, although uneven especially towards the end, is a passionate socialist (but also nationalist) series of novels, with Chris Guthrie as Caledonia herself, suffering but growing through her experiences.

I am thinking of Kinraddie and Grassic Gibbon when I whiz past a war memorial, isolated by this now busy road. And there comes to mind the scene in *Sunset Song*, when Chris attends the dedication of the Kinraddie memorial, made out of a standing stone and including the name of her first husband, who was shot as a deserter. It is as good an evocation of Scotland and Scottish landscape and memories that I have ever read, as well as being a bit of prose that makes one feel the cold wind and the high hill and the emotions of the moment. I look it up when I get home and am touched again by its simplicity:

> *The minister said, Let us pray, and folk took off their hats, it smote cold on your pow. The sun was fleering up in the clouds, it was quiet on the hill, you saw young Chris stand looking down on Kinraddie with her bairn's hand in hers. And then the Lord's Prayer was finished, the minister was speaking just ordinary, he said they had come to honour the folk whom the War had taken, and that the clearing of this ancient site was maybe the memory that best they'd have liked. And he gave a nod to old Brigson and the strings were pulled and off came the clout and there on the Standing Stone the words shone out in their dark grey lettering, plain and*

short: For the Memory of Charles Strachan: James Leslie: Robert Duncan: Ewan Tavendale: who were of this land and fell in the Great War in France: Revelation IICH 28 Verse.

(Which says, of course, 'And I will give them the morning star' – which might be a communist joke, but I think not.)

Grassic Gibbon was less good when he wrote about Aberdeen and its social problems, but inspired when he described the landscape and people he had come from, and their hardships and joys. Even today, with the countryside and its people changed so much, there is still a recognisable hard but sympathetic truth of his words in these places I am passing and in many other parts of rural Scotland.

Soon I am skirting Stonehaven – with its restored outdoor pool, one of the last in Scotland, and beginning to see the outskirts of Aberdeen: retail parks, new housing estates, roads off to industrial sites. Thinking about how this has changed since 1934 (I am told later that it was all farm land, and pretty scrubby and unproductive land at that), I suddenly remember that I have been passing all day through SNP-represented territory: my whole journey has been in a single Euro Constituency represented by the SNP: Perth, Angus and North Tayside (which I have touched the edge of) all have SNP MPs: Perth and Angus too have SNP local authorities. Yet in 1934 there was not a single elected SNP representative in Scotland, at any level of democracy. There are people in parts of this area – in Angus for instance – for whom not being represented by the SNP is unusual: since 1974 they have only had a couple of sessions of a Tory MP and even less of non-SNP local government. Some council wards are on their third successive SNP councillor.

Scotland in1934, in the grip of the depression, was a battleground of political ideas. But those ideas were about economic theory, not about constitutional progress. Or rather the constitutional ideas were very much subsumed by the desperately relevant debate about how to alleviate the nation's poverty. Muir addresses this issue head on in the closing pages of *Scottish Journey*. He analyses the two options for Scotland – nationalism versus socialism (which he describes as being to do with the economic process, either explained by Marx or Major Douglas). He appears sympathetic to some aspects of the national movement: 'if the Nationalists' ideas were put into practice it would no doubt help to redress the inequality between the two countries: the unemployed figures in Scotland would probably decrease...that is assuming the present industrial system continued.' But, he argues, 'the slums would still exist as they are: the great majority of the people would still be poor: the workman would still live in fear of being thrown out of his job.'

The result, he believes would 'no doubt be better than the present state of things, but it does not seem to me an end worth striving for.' And moreover, he criticises the SNP – just born as it then was – for being 'unable to make any pronouncements on the one question which most concerns everybody today, not only in Scotland but in the whole civilised world – the economic question', and observes acidly that 'a movement does not grow by being generally inoffensive but by setting before it an aim more important and definite enough to attract to it an increasing number of supporters.'

Muir prefers the socialist solution of the times – 'the fundamental cause of [Scotland's] many ills, including even the de-nationalisation of its people, [is] economic and not national.' 'I can imagine', he says, 'Scotland freed from Capitalism and using all its rich resources for the good of all its people. A Scotland which achieved that end would be a nation, but it would not care very much whether it was called a nation or not: the problem would have become an academic one. On the other hand, the Scottish qualities which the Nationalists wish to revive artificially would then probably revive of themselves, since the system that has helped most to destroy them would no longer exist.'

But even Muir, even this utopian socialist, admits that the

end he aspires to is 'far away'. He observes on the very last page of *Scottish Journey* that: 'there is no doubt that the Scottish people, with their immense store of potential energy, would be capable of using the resources of modern production to create a society such as I have imagined. An enormous change must happen before that can take place, it is true; but the development of Industrialism itself is driving us towards such a change. The only political question of any importance now is how that development is to be directed, how that transition is to be made.'

And he concludes the book with these words: 'Scotland, with its derelict industries, its vast slums, its depopulated glens, its sweated peasantry, and its army of unemployed, has no future save through such a change. This view may seem at first a depressing one; but to me it seems the only cheerful one.'

Driving into Aberdeen it seems to me at first simply curious that Muir should have devoted so much time and thought to an issue which was not live politically – or at least not at the ballot box – when he wrote. The SNP was only being founded as he wrote, and at the Kilmarnock by-election in November 1933 – the last significant electoral contest before his journey – a nationalist candidate standing jointly for the National Party of Scotland and the Scottish Party had recorded a mere 16% of the vote, coming fourth. That was certainly much better than Eric Linklater's performance in the Fife Eastern division nine months earlier, where Magnus's father got less than 4% and lost his deposit.

Even in the 1935 General Election there were only 8 candidates, five of whom lost their deposits and none of whom came closer than third (although Sir Alastair MacEwan recorded 28% of the vote in the Western Isles). It would be another ten years before there was an SNP MP – and he only for a few weeks. It would be 32 years before the SNP started to have continuous parliamentary representation.

Yet Muir clearly saw the battle lines that were now being drawn. And he stood – as most Scots stand – neither clearly on one side nor the other. It is not the position of Scots and Scotland that has changed over the past 50 years, but the balance of the argument. Muir wanted to see action on derelict industries, on the vast slums, on depopulated glens and 'sweated peasantry', and a solution to the scourge of unemployment. Then, he thought, there would be a nation, though the gaining of that nation would not matter too much to most people.

In a curious way, passing the ever-growing suburbs of Aberdeen, what he predicted then is coming to pass: our derelict industries are no longer with us (coal mining is virtually dead, steel making is gone, shipbuilding is small and specialised), our slums are erased and even the new ones we have created since then in tower blocks and vast estates are being tackled – though slowly. Our glens are still depopulating but at last the issues of land reform and rural survival are on the agenda – and our peasantry is not sweated any longer, usually because there is no rural peasantry as farms and farming become more efficient and yet less profitable. Even unemployment, cyclical as it is, is not at 1930's levels and never has been again – though it looked as if Thatcher might achieve the doubtful honour of taking the figures and the misery back there.

It is not the SNP that has achieved such things – though its pressure and its ability to articulate the Scottish case and put pressure on Westminster to remember it (after all it was not the 11 SNP MPs that mattered in 1974 but the 42 second places, mostly in Labour seats) has certainly been a strong contributory factor. But as Scotland moves into the 21st century it is its belief in itself, and in its better life, that makes it now consider how it should present itself to the world, and how it should be governed. Bad times only lead to change when revolution is the way out; in a country that is not given to revolutionary change, it is the better times that encourage thoughts of progress, and underlie the necessary self-belief.

So in the most curious of ways what I am seeing now around Aberdeen may be the motor for independence and the national status that Muir thought would be fine, but not important. And that too should be an aim – a national movement and a nation that does not see its coming of age as a thing in itself, but only as an incidental happening on the passage to normality. The mistake – if there was one, because mistakes in politics are the fruits of hindsight only – of the early SNP was to put the national question only in terms of nationhood. It must be expressed in terms of normal life, and then it will appear quite normal.

Today I am merely reinforcing my knowledge of Aberdeen in a whistle-stop tour. So before lunch with a broadcasting colleague, I drive round the city, looking at places I am familiar with. My younger brother was at university in the city, and shared a flat for a while with a young and ambitious student called Alastair Darling, of the Darling family that had provided a Tory Lord Provost to Edinburgh. At that time he had a most engaging sense of humour. He and I concocted a column for the Aberdeen University student newspaper (I was visiting while working on a programme in the city) that poked fun at my brother's political ambition, and then vigorously denied authorship to my outraged sibling! My brother was to become sabbatical vice-president and then president of the SRC and was the first student on the university court.

Darling went on to be a passionate left-winger in Edinburgh Labour circles, being one of the causes of my then Edinburgh flatmate to leave the party and join the SDP. But invention, particularly self-invention, being all in Labour circles, now he is the rigorously Blairite rising star of the cabinet and has just been appointed to the thorny Department for Social Security in the reshuffle of late July 1998. I preferred him when he was a human being!

I pass the flat and drive on to Grampian Television (now part of the Scottish Media empire) and then back along Union Street, all the time conscious of the regimentation of Aberdeen's buildings – the granite city may be a tourist appellation, but it gives the place a grey, cold look. Granite is the most unyielding of rocks.

Aberdeen is a working-class city surrounded by rural Scotland. Certainly it has pushed its way out in recent years, and grown wealthy on the black gold off its shores. But it feels no more hospitable than it felt when I first came here – there is still a snell wind that blows through the town, and dark corners by the harbour that make passers-by walk more quickly.

Old Aberdeen is bonny and bright – the heart of the university, and full of interesting small shops. And some of the new suburbs have a touch more thought in their layout than is normal in Scotland. Though Muir did not think it worthwhile to come here, I am glad I have and I want to find out more about what makes the city work, and what it thinks the parliament might do.

I have arranged lunch with an acquaintance who works for the BBC. We sit in a fashionable small restaurant, the tables full on a working-day lunchtime, though having looked at the menu prices I am glad he is picking up the tab. He is from the city, though his Aberdeen accent has faded somewhat. Most Scots know Doric, as it is called, only from the humour of that priceless trio who call their shows 'Scotland the What' and from Robbie Shepherd, who hosts a Scottish dance-band show on Radio Scotland. It is hard, for those who are not familiar with it, to penetrate it at times, but it has a lilt – and a bluntness – all of its own.

My acquaintance is scathing about the political future of Scotland. He sees the parliament as being a creation of the industrial central belt, and wonders if Aberdeen and the North-east will get a look in. 'Look at it this way', he says, 'we'll have three MSPs from the city, and three more from the area – and perhaps if we're lucky a couple from the regional list. Glasgow alone will have sixteen or seventeen – and then there's Lanarkshire, and Renfrew and all those places. The parliament won't control the oil industry and fishing here is almost dead. We'll be lucky to be thought about every third month!' Paradoxically he is an enthusiast for more change – for fuller tax powers and (perhaps) for full independence.

'Then', he adds, 'we might be more important, because we will have the oil and we can make a noise.'

Contrary to what people think, the oil industry is not on the decline in the North-east. 'There is as much to come out as we have taken already – perhaps more', he says as he warms to the theme. 'Technology is improving all the time – all that is holding us back at the moment is the low oil price. When the price rises, as it will, then it will become economic again to go to the margins, and to start to look north and west for even more fields.'

But he is keen to stress what Aberdeen has to offer apart from oil: 'This is a great city, a great place to live...[it has started to rain as we talk, and the windows are shaking with the gusts that are battering the city]... its got countryside all around, and the mix of people – Americans, French, other Europeans, English – its wakened the place up.' He tells me of a dinner party he was at two nights ago, when conversation ranged from American politics to French policing, to Estonian folk customs – all topics informed by people who actually came from these places.

'Scotland can be a great place if it remembers that there is more than the central belt, and if it looks out across the North Sea instead of just south to England. Aberdeen had more trading links with Russia than the rest of the country put together before the First World War – and it was the war that ruined those. We can rebuild our Eastern links if we choose to do so.'

Over the coffee I ask him what he wants – wants personally – from the parliament. He pauses for a long time before admitting to one obsession: the waste of resources that is the result of current private land-ownership in the Highlands and the North-east. 'I want to see a new approach to how we use our land', he says. 'I want the people of the estates to have a say in what happens to them.' He tells me of a story he has done recently about a large swathe of land in the West, where the land has been bought and sold several times between companies, and where the community does not know from one day to the next who actually owns the feus to their houses or the hill on which they graze their sheep.

'People think that the Clearances and the abuse of tenants is something from the past. But on smaller scale it still goes on. Land is a resource, and it should be used for the benefit of the people themselves. What does the Gaelic proverb say – the people are mightier than a Lord? If that parliament does anything, it has to make that saying come true.'

We shake hands on the pavement, the bill (thankfully) in his pocket. I had thought of him before as a typical journalist, if there is such a thing. But there is a belief in him that things can get better, though a scepticism that mere politicians (particularly politicians from the south) can achieve what he wants. That is not an uncommon cynicism – and we have only one chance now to put it right.

It is almost mid-afternoon, but I still have two hours of driving at least before I reach Inverness. The rain has set in, and the traffic leaving Aberdeen is heavy. My windscreen wipers click-clack as I slowly leave the city behind, but this road is not an easy one, and overtaking in this weather is not to be recommended. It is, my trusty little Psion computer tells me, 103.7 miles from Aberdeen to Inverness, and the journey, it asserts, should take me exactly two hours, twelve minutes and fifty seconds. Fond as I am of this miracle of technology – I am a geek, in IT terms, because of my fondness for anything that can automate and inform – from time to time I get a bit irritated by its precision. Why not two hours, thirteen minutes, and call it quits?

Kintore goes past, then the wonderfully named Kirkton of Culsalmond. At Keith I stop to compare my progress with my electronic map. I am about half an hour behind time, so I press on through Fochabers, past the Baxter's foods factory, through Elgin, Lhanbryde and Alves and into Nairn. My two hours are up, and I am still half an hour from Inverness. I am also, in the Scots word, wabbit, tired of driving behind lorries and wiping the mist from screen in front of me. My back is sore too, and I am – if not closing my eyes – at least blinking more often. If I don't stop for a break, I shall be reduced to winding the window down, and driving in the cold rain and wind to keep me awake.

My wife's uncle lived in Nairn for a while, and she is fond of it. To me it is a bit like Troon where I grew up, and my mental map of Troon keeps superimposing itself, so that I find myself startled at street corners, trying to make sense of where I am. We have stayed here on a couple of occasions with friends, most recently with the Lochheads and Dyers (who were our neighbours in Tillietudlem) in a house that Dougie Lochhead inherited.

We spent a weekend practising for a holiday that we all planned to spend together in France, but we were really just drinking and talking and keeping off politics. Nobody got injured, unlike the actual event in France a month later, where Dougie walked into a pillar in the rented villa in the middle of the last night (drink may have been the culprit) and appeared in the final photographs not as the Sean Connery look-alike he thinks he is, but with a Mickey Mouse plaster from the first-aid kit right in the centre of his forehead.

Today I find a wee café and have a tea and a scone – staple Scottish wet summer fare. The English couple at the next table are sitting in dripping cagoules, tensely swapping monosyllables. She, it turns out, wants to drive home to Birkenhead tonight: he fancies staying on and waiting for the weather to clear. She never wanted to come to Scotland in the first place – he had always wanted to come and thinks it would look great, if the mist lifted.

Slowly I am drawn in to arbitrate.

'Will it clear up?' she asks.

'Well it might – the forecast says it will be showery tomorrow. But you never know here – this is a dry spot in Scotland, and rain doesn't last long.'

'But we want to go to Skye tomorrow – will it be drier there?'

A diplomatic pause (nine times out of ten that I have been in Skye, you can't even see the Cuillins). 'It could be – there's a high out in the Atlantic, and it might be in the west by, well, sometime tomorrow.' I fear my attempts at reassurance have not worked: as they leave his wife is scrabbling about for her cheque book and muttering about paying the B&B before they go. I add meteorology to the needs for our forthcoming ministry responsible for tourism.

The last bit of the road to Inverness is easier – I am fresher and I know it well. Soon I am past the turn-off for Inverness airport, past Ardersier where they build oil rigs (when the market is right) and onto a new stretch of dual carriageway fronting a massive retail park that has sprung up since the last time I drove past. Then it is Inverness for real – familiar and comforting. I am back on Muir's route now – though soon I will leave it for good, because I have decided to go over to the Western Isles and then back home to Argyll, whereas Muir headed north by way of the far north-west coastline to a different home – Orkney.

Muir stopped in Inverness for only a short while, preferring to spend the night in Beauly, which he chose because it was a 'smaller town'. That process of differentiation has continued apace – Inverness is now the largest town in the Highlands, while poor Beauly and its like have grown far less quickly. Muir found Inverness 'inconveniently crowded with vehicles of all kinds, most of them stationary'. Traffic has always been an Inverness problem, probably even before the invention of the motor car. But the city fathers don't let the problem get them down: it seems that almost daily they have a new solution, with one-way streets changing direction and new obstacles springing up whenever you visit. Finding a way through Inverness has become almost like an arcade game, with every new year producing a different level of difficulty on which to compete.

I take my time and meander into the centre, cutting back on myself so that I can enjoy the places I know. Cathleen and I lived on the shores of Loch Ness for a year, and worked in the city centre, driving in every day. It was a happy experience, for we were young and energetic and ambitious and it is the place I most regret leaving – a decision forced on me by redundancy and the need to earn a living. Despite some mistakes – a massive shopping mall and the ugly fortified headquarters of what was the Highlands and Islands Development Board and is now Highlands and Islands Enterprise – Inverness has been generally responsible in its expansion and development. The centre is bustling and attractive, with a particularly fine covered market, full of stalls and kiosks that sell an amazing range of products. A hotel manager friend – a Frenchman – once told me of doing six months training in Inverness in the early 1960s and having to scour the market for garlic. Eventually he located a wee Italian, an ex-prisoner of war, who grew some for his own consumption and who readily agreed to part with his surplus to a person who actually knew what to do with it. Today there is exotic produce from all over the world: superb fresh fish and seafood that is sourced closer to home; footwear and sports clothing; a barber's and a bookies – everything you might need under one roof. Even solicitors' offices are apparent in case a quickie divorce is on your list when you're out shopping.

University friends of mine own one of these law practices, but today I have to move on quickly so I don't call on them and find myself invited to stay in their lovely old house overlooking the river and the town. Instead I drive across the river and – the rain having eased off (enough to keep my Nairn tourists in town, I wonder?) – I park and walk along the riverbank. I must have a fascination for water – Dumfries, Perth and Inverness are amongst my favourite towns and all have a strong river running through them. This one is so strong that it brought down the railway bridge some years ago, and in spate it can run almost level with the roads on its banks in the town centre. Standing by the Eden Court theatre, the castle and the town look compact and fresh – washed by the day's downpour, they are now illuminated by a weak sun that is peaking through the clouds.

Inverness calls itself the 'Capital of the Highlands' and it has a Highland feel – Muir describes that as being one in which there is 'a sense of having a great deal of time and space to do what I like with', and I know what he means. It is a feeling that, in me, grows more intense the closer I get to the Western Isles but I can already sense its tug. Usually the most organised of individuals, I feel no need to decide now where I will eat this evening, and who I will see. It is enough to be able to walk the streets, look in the shops, browse amongst the books that I find in Waterstone's or James Thin's (formerly that great Highland bookshop, Melven's) and perhaps drop in to one of the pubs where I am bound to meet someone I know.

I will not seek out the tea rooms that were Muir's forte – still less the tea room here in which he failed to find the 'charged thundery heaviness composed of unresolved desire from which the lightning of an aggressive or a provocative glance might flash at any moment', and instead recognised after a time an atmosphere made up of a 'strange lack of insistence...something contained and yet free, detached and yet spontaneous which seemed so impervious to all desire to draw attention to itself that it conveyed a faint sense of defeat.'

Those phrases have seemed almost meaningless to me until I find myself in the Highlands, and then suddenly – now – I understand what he is trying to say. For the Highlands are a place in which the obsession to be recognised and seen is curiously out of place – there are more important human priorities. Yet it is also a place which knows that the virtues of self-control and confident self-knowledge are little prized elsewhere.

But this is not what Muir made of it. It is not Avilion, 'Where falleth neither sleet nor snow nor any rain...' as he makes out. It is perhaps a place that is simply more rooted in the need for human relations to be real and lasting: a place where the temporal and the fickle will not do. People here have to rely on one another, and such reliance and trust and correct assessment of one's fellow men and women is vital. That made be an old-fashioned thing, of less and less relevance in our modern world where we are all individuals and where permanent alliances are seen to slow us down. But the internal strength it gives might be of more relevance than that which those from furth of here have learnt. It might be something whose time is coming again.

The Highland virtues may not be in everyone that I pass in the street here as I make my way for a drink. But there are still bred in the bone hereabouts. They will be more and more evident as I travel west to the Islands and on to rural Argyll. They make me more comfortable, perhaps because they are strong enough to take our changing society in their stride – as long as we start to show how much we value them and how much we are determined to bring them back to the forefront of our national life.

Chapter Nine
The Highlands and the Isle of Skye

Even after 20 years of travelling to the Western Isles, setting off to go there always gives me a kick of excitement. Having come from Inverness, I feel I am really starting my journey – for sentimental reasons – at the village of Foyers that sits on the southern shore of Loch Ness (or the eastern shore if you prefer accurate geography – Loch Ness sits astride one of the major fault lines across Scotland, and is orientated from eight o'clock to two o'clock).

For a year in the early 1980s Cathleen and I lived here – in one of about 30 flats and houses that surround that most untypical of Scottish of features, a village green. This is in Upper Foyers and the houses were originally built to house workers at the aluminium extraction plant that opened in the village in 1896. Lower Foyers sits on the loch side down a very steep hill: it is also one of the most popular 'monster hunting' sites and we used to have a neighbour who claimed to have felt a huge rough flipper touch her and disturb the water when she was swimming from this spot.

The much more prosaic aluminium plant close by was supplied with electricity by Scotland's first commercial hydro-electric scheme which harnessed the potential energy of the Falls of Foyers as its power source. Although the factory closed in the late 60s, there is still a power station here – one of the many that uses hydro power to supply the North of Scotland with electricity. Indeed the former public electricity utility – now privatised – was called the North of Scotland Hydro-Electric Board.

Lord Kelvin was the consultant on the first Foyers scheme, but what engineers propose sometimes takes politicians to implement. The great Tom Johnston (his name again – when Muir was writing he had not even become Regional Commissioner for Scotland, to which post he was appointed at the start of the Second World War, becoming Secretary of State in 1941) created the board in 1945, showing considerable political skill in persuading the Highlands that industrialisation of the type he wished would not destroy the landscape, but would instead raise the standard of living and the potential of an area that had been exporting people rather than anything else for two centuries.

Johnston took over the chairmanship of the board when it was formed in 1945 and continued in the post until 1959 – at the helm of what he saw as the economic powerhouse of the Highlands. Johnston's wartime administration of Scotland is remembered so positively not just for his achievements, but for how he operated. Given the emergency he would have got away with autocracy and diktat: instead he set up a Scottish Council of State which comprised all the living holders of his office. That body guaranteed cross-party support and allowed Johnston to innovate and change while taking Scotland with him. Perhaps we should name our new parliament building – or some part of it – after Johnston as a living reminder that political consensus and agreement is not only possible in Scotland but can also deliver results!

Johnston had every reason to be mired in the political dogfight. A working journalist he was Keir Hardie's campaign manager during an unsuccessful rectorial contest. Campaign managers tend to be the most partisan of figures, planning not just how to win, but also how to defeat their opponents. He entered parliament in 1922 at the second attempt, only to lose his West Stirlingshire seat in 1924. He won a Dundee by-election in 1925, took his original seat back in 1929 and within the next two years had held junior office in Scotland and then a cabinet post as Lord Privy Seal. Yet he lost again in 1931, but bounced back as member for the same constituency in 1935 and held it until 1945 when he left politics – refusing a peerage as he did so.

Anyone who lost three of his seven election campaigns in the space of just over 20 years might be entitled to a bit of battle weariness, and a tendency to the simplicities of being a political bruiser. To have resisted that temptation and to have the vision to see the need for consultation and persuasion marks Johnston out as an exceptional modern political figure. So does his firm rejection of ennoblement, usually the last compromise with principle that a democratic politician, or a rising businessman, makes.

The time for people like Tom Johnston is coming round again. Politicians who can survive in the hurly burly of elections but who can also put such activities to one side when the responsibility of power beckons, and seek the common weel by consensus and leadership. I have no doubt that such skills are what the people of Scotland want to see applied to their parliament – the fact they are harder than ever to achieve as two parties with many similarities (at least in Scotland) fight for supremacy on the narrow ground of Caledonian politics should not mean they are unattainable; merely difficult to sustain in the face of one's rivals fears, and one's own party's history and ambitions.

During the year we spent in Foyers we only walked to its most famous feature – the Falls – a couple of times. They were 'discovered' by distinguished travellers once General Wade's military road on the south side of Loch Ness was built in the 18th century (the main road now runs on the northern side, bustling with frustrated tourist traffic throughout its length). Dr Johnson was nervous about the dangers of getting close to their 'dreadful depth': Burns visited and recorded them in some unmemorable lines. The most celebrated description comes from Christopher North (the pen name of John Wilson, writer, lawyer, friend of Wordsworth and Coleridge, Professor of Moral Philosophy – although he got a friend to do his work for that one) who called the Falls 'the most magnificent cataract in Britain' and who advised his readers that it was 'worth walking a thousand miles to behold them'.

The harnessing of the falls has reduced their power, but the visit is still worthwhile. As with many Scottish natural attractions, there has been an improvement over the past 15 years in the directions to them and in the information available to visitors. But more could still be done – because in this small village on the quiet side of Loch Ness there lies not only a significant part of our industrial heritage, but also a way of connecting to some of the great minds of the 19th century.

The road into Foyers passes Boleskine House, until recently owned by rock guitarist Jimmy Page (who apparently was sighted in the vicinity as often as his near neighbour in the loch) but once the home of the notorious occultist Aleister Crowley – 'The Beast' – who gained notoriety not just for his bad and frightening novels, but also for alleged necromancy. The road in front of the house separates the property from a small cemetery: the juxtaposition is more than a little sinister, and locals still advise a touch of acceleration, and certainly no dallying late at night in a storm.

The road out is much more welcoming: it sweeps down into a river valley and then twists and turns for several miles through woodlands and past the river, which has inviting flat banks in places. When it opens out, it joins the road that has come from behind the high ground on which Foyers perches overlooking the loch and then rises up through lochs and moorland until dropping suddenly into the wee town of Fort Augustus. Before the 1715 rising there was only a tiny hamlet at this southern end of Loch Ness. A barracks was built at that time but the great Fort (where Dr Johnson – my path is crossing his now – had the 'best night's sleep in his life') was only erected in 1730, as the hub of the network of military roads whose creation was the means by which the Highlands could be kept in check, should that be required again.

The 'Augustus' whom Wade honoured in naming the place was none other than William Augustus, Duke of Cumberland, who was to visit the place 16 years later, and used it as his base for completing the vicious rout and persecution of those who supported (or who might have supported, or whom others believed supported, or who just looked as if they could have supported) Charles Edward Stuart.

As I drive down the hill, I can see through the trees just by the loch the Abbey of Fort Augustus, which is built on the foundations of the fort, and which is a better use of the land. The Abbey was best known as a catholic boarding school, founded in 1878 – the actual abbey foundation is a few years later – but now the school has gone, and the monks are in sole possession of their gothic building, or rather in sole possession along with the tourists, who are encouraged as the only cash crop hereabouts.

It was a Lord Lovat who bought the Fort and gave it to the Benedictines. That old catholic family's fortunes have fallen and risen again and again in the Highlands: in Beauly, the little town where Muir chose to stay instead of Inverness, he visited the old church, which had been on the family lands and which was part of the estate which they forfeited after they had backed the wrong Jacobite horse. Their wealth grew again in the 19th century, but by the end of this one the family fortunes are in decline again and their magnificent house, Beauly Castle has had to be sold to pay off the duties which have befallen the family after a string of bizarre occurrences. That it was bought by the richest woman in Scotland, Anne Gloag (a former nurse who, along with her brother Brian Souter, has not only known hard times as well but also possesses an unerring eye for business and a determination to succeed that is still too rare in Scotland), is somewhat poetic in the circumstances.

But despite the popularity of some of the braver members of the Lovat family, most have precious few tears to shed for the decline of the Highland gentry. One of the main reasons for this becomes apparent as soon as I have left Fort Augustus, driving along the Caledonian Canal.

This is a fertile valley, but it supports only a tiny population. Since leaving Inverness the only two significant inhabited areas I have passed through have owed their existence to 18th and 19th-century events: Fort Augustus to the 'settlement' of the intransigent population and Foyers, over a hundred years later, to power generation. Together they probably do not house more than 1500 people – and I have driven almost 40 miles. Add another 500 for the occasional house or farm, and we are still travelling through one of the least populated parts of Scotland. Travel further north and further west, though, and even this density takes on the semblance of a metropolis.

To many who come here as tourists – to some even who decide to stay – the attraction of the Highlands is precisely this emptiness: the fact that the landscape is not dominated by people and that it is still possible to live in harmony with nature, and feel and see its impact. That is also possible in other places in Scotland – Galloway, South Ayrshire, the Borders – but nowhere else is it so possible, in so great a space. Above the Great Glen there lies almost half of Scotland's land mass: but it contains less than ten percent of its people.

But that number could be doubled without any great detrimental impact on the landscape. Indeed, using sensible and sensitive technologies it would be possible to increase the population and actually protect more effectively that landscape and the way of life. The flat and endless acres of moorland are not all a natural phenomenon: they are the sign of depredation, exhaustion by sheep, overgrazing by a deer population that is far larger than the land can sustain – and also a sign of neglect. The present paucity of human population is similarly unnatural and the result of human intervention.

That depopulation has been dramatic. It has also been continuous since the mid-18th century, and it continues today. Of course because there are far less people living in the

Highlands and Islands, the size of the decrease is much smaller than it has been – but it has not yet been arrested in most places. I can stand in my wife's home township in North Uist and count the population down – almost down and out – over the next generation. Inverness and Stornoway may grow: so may some of the villages with houses bought by those who wish to retire, or perhaps who want a better life than can be found in Camberwell or Cumbernauld. The place, I accept, will never be empty – but equally it will never start to fill up.

The circumstances of the Highland Clearances are too well known to bear much repetition here: save to say that their bitter memory may not be on everyone's lips, but their sad effect remains in most hearts. It has to, because its living history is all around and cannot be escaped. Its legacy lies in each acre, in each township – not just in piles of stones that once were houses, but in the very fact that on a November evening there are three people in the bar of the local hotel, on a January morning half of every family party will be leaving for their real home after a Hogmanay visit, and on any day there is no bus, no train, no travelling shop, because there are no customers worth servicing.

Dennis MacLeod – an exile returned to the Highlands having made his fortune – is involved in many different projects. But one that is closest to his heart is to create a memorial to the Clearances that will draw a line under the bitterness and anger and help with the process of regeneration. He has a vision of the exiles sending something from their new country to form part of the exhibition, indeed part of the fabric of the structure itself: stone perhaps from Canada, New Zealand, South Africa, America.

Such a memorial would have three purposes: the first is to ensure that what happened is not forgotten; that in the cause of economic progress virtually a whole population was deprived of what they thought was their land – deprived indeed of their very homes and sometimes of any possessions they could not carry away – and sent thousands of miles to start a new life in a strange land.

The second would be to remind Scotland and the world that a society that thinks only of economic progress – only of the fashionable theories of the moment – can inflict terrible wrongs on innocent people. Muir puts it well when considering the same topic. 'It is difficult now to understand why the Duke of Sutherland, who seems to have been a kind and enlightened man, should have rooted out a whole people with such barbarity. It was mainly, I think, because at that time intelligent men's minds were possessed by a dream of general wealth for society, which would be realised by adhering to the latest economic principles...' Muir calls this a 'Utopian passion'. But he goes on to make a vital link: 'It is this particular ideal of progress that has depopulated the Highlands and reduced them to the status of a backward region. They were robbed of their life by the exactly the same process that built Glasgow.'

Unfettered dreams of economic progress are never an unmixed blessing. They create some winners, and perhaps in time they create a general betterment of society. But they also create some categories of losers – the victims of the Clearances *and* the Glasgow slum dwellers. History does not have to repeat itself, particularly if lessons are learnt, rather than slavish example followed. Scotland as a nation has an international perspective – it has nothing to fear from globalisation if it prepares itself well. But when 'globalisation' is seen as the latest, most attractive, most-likely-to-be-successful economic theory, and when politicians start to say that in order for 'globalisation' to be achieved there will be the need for some people to suffer – then think again of the Clearances and impress upon politicians the fact that suffering can spread wide and deep and surface in unexpected places. Two hundred redundancies in one place because of the need for competitiveness may result in 100 people elsewhere who become the new underclass of the 'information poor'.

This lesson of the Clearances is not that change should not happen – it is that change has to be a human process, not just an economic one. And that even 'kind and enlightened' men – perhaps especially 'kind and enlightened' men – are dangerous if they are enthused merely with the need for change, rather than with the general desire to spread their kindness and light to all around.

The third purpose of remembering the Clearances is to awake in the minds of those who live here – and more importantly those who don't – the realisation of the potential of the Highlands and Islands. Some weeks before I travelled this road I met with one of the prime movers of a putative 'Highland Alliance' – a prototype for a political party that would seek to represent the Highlands in the new parliament. I have a lot of admiration for the some of the individuals involved in this idea. They are people who are deeply committed to the communities they know and love: they want to see the best for such communities and they feel that politics often gets in the way of direct representation.

I would also not question for a moment their sincere belief that the Highlands have been neglected by Westminster (it is a fact) and that some of the political structures that may exist at Holyrood might perpetuate such neglect, if they copy Westminster patterns. Yet they are wrong on two counts: wrong because if Scotland starts to fragment now then the parliament will be too weak to actually address any of the problems they are concerned with. And wrong because the problems of the Highlands, distinct as they may be, are not all or even mostly unique.

Certainly the Clearances have left a stain which has weakened economic and social progress. And certainly there needs to be new thinking about development in the Highlands – not just knee-jerk reaction to environmental threats, followed by plaintive hand wringing when yet another crisis hits forestry or fishing or crofting. But such new thinking does not have to involve just Highlanders. A parliament – an independent parliament – that does not think about the Highlands will be one that fails, and fails because it has not thought about how to get the best out of the whole of the country for the betterment of the whole of the country.

For example Denis MacLeod glows with enthusiasm about creating a new population centre in Caithness or Sutherland – a centre that can create one of the natural harbours on the northern coastline, invest in alternative energy and attract a new population to bring life to that area. By creating, too, a counterbalance to Inverness such a development might open up the North-west and encourage sustainable and sensitive change in the whole area. The prototype for this idea lies in the establishment of Dounreay in the 50s – but all that was created then was a company town and an environmental hazard that could still blight our future. We should have learned that lesson, and be prepared to invest that learning in another chance to rebuild part of the Highlands. But this plan cannot be brought to fruition by the Highlands alone. It needs a political consensus, an element of national economic planning, inclusion in the transport infrastructure – and a determination to make it work that must lie at least as much in Edinburgh, and in Brussels, as in Inverness, Golspie or Wick.

A real nation would also make certain that the issues of transport, jobs, housing, health, education and the environment were priorities for all its areas, urban and rural. The particulars of these matters for the Highlands are Highland issues – but the general issues are Scottish, European and global ones. A 'Highland Party' might have all these things on its priority list – but it will still fall short of what the Highlands need, because the Highlands need to lead and influence Scotland, to teach Scotland (and the world) some of the lessons of its past, and build with Scotland a better society for everyone. And if it weakened the Highland voice in the other parties – if the other parties decided to prioritise elsewhere because they had become 'Lowland', or 'East-coast' parties by default – then it would weaken the whole idea of our parliament.

Months ago Dr Finlay MacLeod – a real 'Highland activist' if there ever was one – raised with me the question of the need for the parliament to think differently about the Highlands, the Islands and Gaelic; to be a place which provided solutions by negotiation and discussion and which would become a democratic institution owned by the whole of the country. He saw the parliament as an opportunity, not a threat; something to be made use of, rather than something that – even before it opens – people are organising against, fearful of *'mir nan mor nan Gall'** (to quote the Gaelic saying). It would be best to put away at the start the divisiveness that – quite unwittingly I am sure – any 'Highland Party' would create, and instead enlist our new democracy as a positive partner in putting right so much that is wrong.

The slight mood of gloom that thoughts of the Clearances can create (anyone with a knowledge of Scottish history is conditioned to it) is matched by the gloomy early summer – one of the worst in recent memory. Rain is falling again as I turn right at Invergarry and start the slow climb up and across to the main Inverness/Skye road, the 'Road to the Isles'. As the road breasts the summit between the two glens I cannot even see the loch that lies below – a loch that from this spot has an outline very reminiscent of the shape of Scotland itself.

I pull in for a moment by the cairn that commemorates Willie MacRae. There is another car there, and I vaguely recognise the young couple in it. They are party members, passing on a holiday trip and we talk a little about the curious happenings that took place here: the supposed accidental death in 1985 of a well-known and senior Nationalist (who also was a Zionist and a passionate anti-nuclear campaigner), the finding of the body by another up-and-coming Nationalist who happened to be passing; the very tardy discovery by the police of a bullet wound in his head; the bizarre theory that he could have shot himself dead and then thrown the gun away; the allegation of a sighting of a man with a rifle on a nearby hillside and the inevitable rumour factory that produced more and more unanswerable suppositions about what had transpired. We agree that the truth will probably never be known; we also agree that it is time the Crown Office agreed to publish all its documents so that at least the wilder ideas can

* 'The great hatred of the Southerner'.

be discounted. And with those agreements, we allow each other a bit of space and silence to stand by the stones that were brought here by Nationalists from all over Scotland and wonder anew at what this wild, windswept, wet place actually witnessed.

The drive on to Skye is made even gloomier by this stop. The rain has set in again and I hope that the English tourists from the tea shop in Nairn decided to go home – that way they might keep a little curiosity for a better day. At least the traffic is light – though that also probably signifies that it really is a bad tourist season. On a good day one can glimpse the Skye Bridge from afar and be amazed by its ethereal beauty – a trace of elegant white, arching into the Highland landscape. But today I am almost at Kyle before I can see it – and it looks as dreich as everything else.

For the last ten miles I have been wondering whether I should refuse to pay at the toll booths, adding myself to the long list of those who object in the strongest terms not just to the imposition of yet another economic disadvantage for the islands, but also at the obscenely one-sided arrangement by which the bridge was built, which as more and more information emerges seems to be risk-free for the Bank of America, but costly for everyone else.

I cop out of civil disobedience at the last moment, deciding that the hassle on this time-pressured journey is going to be too much. I have a ferry to catch at Uig, but I make a mental apology to those who have blazed the trail, and a mental note to promise to do it at some stage in the future. To salve my conscience I tell the toll operator (nicely) that I object to paying: he doesn't even blink an eyelid. He just replies with the all-purpose Scottish 'Aye'.

The experience of driving the brief distance from the mainland to the islands is an amazing one. Most bridges go straight across, or are buttressed so that there is no real feeling of height. But this bridge rises up, and sweeps round to Skye, giving on a clear day a wonderful view to the north-west and south. The feeling of fragility is intense – I suspect it also leads to a sudden slowing down, least you leave this construction in mid-stream and find yourself hurtling down into the water far below.

I have no doubt that Skye is better off with this bridge than with a thousand ferries, shuttling across the Kyles. But equally, if we believe in opening up the Highlands and drawing them into the benefits of modern Scotland, we should not do so by the imposition of tolls. Ferry fares are already too high – and where a cost has to be met because there is no alternative, it would be best to set that cost as low as possible. Roads are massively subsidised, so shouldn't an essential road like this also be a public service, rather than an expensive private fiefdom with a captive market?

Muir, of course, had gone north as well but not this far west, but he had his experience of ferry crossings – not just to Orkney, but at Kylesku, where he 'had to wait three hours for the tide'. It is better to travel like this – and on improved roads and faster ferries – than to experience that. But as this world becomes one in which we (or what we need) has to travel it would be good if 'travel poverty' did not become (as it is becoming) yet another form of social exclusion.

Skye is a larger island than I am used to – the more domestic pleasures of Uist and Benbecula await ahead, so I drive through without stopping, affected also by my usual paranoia about missing boats and trains that always ends up with me being the first one waiting on the pier, or at the station. I pass the old school that was once the headquarters of the *West Highland Free Press*, that scourge of both the Highland laird and the distant local authority when it was founded by a young radical journalist called Brian Wilson. In keeping with his upward mobility it is now a restaurant (a rather good one, actually, but only open in the summer). The paper is now produced from an industrial unit on the Portree side of Broadford

In the late 1970s I wrote the occasional article for the Free Press, admiring its strong pro-Highland stance and its not so gentle pricking of egos and cronyism. Along with other forces, such as the 7:84 theatre company (7% of the population own 84% of the wealth) it created a climate for change in an area that for a century had espoused radical politics but accepted ultra conservative land laws and doffed its cap to feudalism. And no matter how much it was raged against by the establishment (perhaps because it was raged against by the establishment) it survived through thin financial times.

There is still a shadow of its former self to be seen each week when it comes out, and is bought throughout the islands and in many places on the mainland – including the paper shop next door to my office. But it has also fallen prey to the changes in its former proprietor: it pursues strange and vicious vendettas, often against Nationalists and it can find itself as an apologist for the most reactionary of New Labour policies. Its arteries have hardened and its cheeky and sharp observation now seems (at times) dogmatic and even unpleasant.

Wilson himself, as a government minister, takes no direct part in the running of the paper. His weekly column has been passed over to someone else (a pity as at times Brian has the type of pen that one imagines Christopher North possessed – dipped in acid but capable of great entertainment) and his bile now overflows at the despatch box in the House of Commons or in press and television interviews. And the bile is less and less entertaining and more and more dangerous to successful Scottish politics. Consider this, from the *Herald* in July 1998, commenting on the pressure from the SNP for the release of a report on Scottish Studies in the educational curriculum:

The idea that political nationalism and the promotion of Scottish culture are synonymous is offensive. Offhand I can't think of a Nationalist politician whose knowledge of Scottish culture extends much beyond the first verse of Flower of Scotland and even then they don't understand its historical context.

For a start no one had ever suggested that nationalism and the promotion of Scottish culture are synonymous. Indeed I have gone out of my way to say that such a correspondence would be stupid. Charitably this opening shot might be considered a smokescreen: uncharitably it is a brazen lie, for it implies something has been said which has not been said. Yet it gets worse. Wilson, of course, can think of a dozen Nationalists or more who were or are significant forces in, and experts on, Scottish culture. Paul Scott is the editor of the definitive modern reader on the subject; Douglas Young was a prominent SNP member and office bearer, and a respected Scottish poet; Hugh MacDiarmid himself was a member of the party, but the remark is designed not be an accurate assessment, but a denigration. And such denigration is then finished off with a flourish: an attack on a popular song (not just for Nationalists – it was played as the national anthem at all Scottish World Cup football matches and is even played at Murrayfield, the sporting temple of the Scottish middle class) and an implication that Nationalists know nothing of their nation's history (or otherwise, Wilson is saying, they wouldn't be Nationalists).

154

The whole statement is self-indulgent rubbish, but it is deliberately made. It expresses not just a hatred for Nationalists, but the desire that everyone should see and agree with that hatred. Over the past few years I have been much struck by what could be called the 'rhetoric gap'. Michael Forsyth was given to excesses of patriotism in his speeches – during the disastrous relaunch of the Scottish Conservatives under the slogan 'Be a Patriot, not a nationalist' – which would have been howled down at any SNP conference from any speaker – and howled down not just by the press but by party members. Wilson regularly uses language that for me would be grounds for dumping the most junior of candidates or the most senior of spokespeople. George Robertson – another old-time Nat-hunter, who had been a member of the party when young (just as Wilson was) – called the SNP 'snake oil salesmen' at the Labour Conference in Perth in 1998 and got a standing ovation! And Blair has been sucked into the trap, substituting 'separatists' and 'separatism' for the words we use about ourselves and by which Scotland knows us.

Some believe that these actions are self-defeating: they certainly seem to have no negative effect on the SNP. But they do have an effect on the public perception of politicians, and the public response to politics. Scotland says again and again that it wants constructive, co-operative government – and an end to the Westminster schoolyard. Yet the more it is said, the more that Labour in particular now resort to this sort of verbal abuse. Passionate rhetoric is understandable. Humorous micky-taking is effective. Lies, slanders and insults contribute nothing, however, except to lower politics in public esteem just at the time when its profile needs to be raised, and the willing involvement of every Scot sought in the task of creating a new parliament.

When Brian was a journalist he spoke as a journalist. Now, however, it is time for him to put away childish things. To the extent that he has failed so far, then he has failed to become the politician he always aspired to be.

I am now past the road to Armadale, Isleornsay and the Gaelic college at Sabhal Mor Ostaig, and through Broadford, the spiritual home of Drambuie. This whole southern part of Skye mixes strong Gaelic culture, and a keen desire to preserve it and build upon it, with home-counties tourism and an increasing settlement of non-Gaelic speakers. Surprisingly it seems not to cause conflict, but to stir a productive pot and infect each side with a sense of balance, and a desire to learn.

The long centre of Skye also goes past quickly. I wish I had time to turn off and see my four nieces and nephews at Struan, and my brother-in-law who farms there. Perhaps later in the summer I can come back and take up a friendship I value (though such procrastination tends to erode relationships, not intensify them). But I need to be through Portree and over the hill to Uig in an hour and a half – plenty of time unless you share my fear of missing ferries.

Plenty of time indeed – I am driving down to Uig bay before the boat has even arrived from Uist. The rain has cleared and clouds lifted – there is a faint line on the horizon which I know is the Western Isles: Further north Muir had glimpsed the 'long misty outline of Lewis' before turning eastwards again and had reflected on the 'small rocky islets' that lay in the numerous bays on that coastline. He found them 'impervious to all the sentimental associations which nature usually evokes in one's mind' and even when he turned to the small houses on the hill land above him, he still retained an 'impression of strangeness'.

I have the opposite feelings every time I get here. Although I was brought up somewhere very different, Uig always feels to me as the gateway to home: the long final mile that will take me to where I really belong. Far from being impervious to sentimental associations, this little bay, and the seascape that is revealed as the boat turns out from it, seems overflowing with them.

Chapter Ten
The Islands of the Stranger

The waters that we are starting to cross have seen – and still see
– a huge variety of traffic. Today to the north I can see an oil
tanker, taking the more sheltered route from Shetland down
the Scottish coast: its alternative way lies on the Atlantic side
of this chain of islands. On its current course it carries a risk of
collision or grounding that might have catastrophic conse-
quences for the environment. When the *Braer* sank off
Shetland some years ago there was much talk of trying to stop
tankers using the Minch – not much seems to have come of it.
Doubtless there will have to be an incident before anything
gets done. Perhaps this is one sort of problem that Holyrood
could sort out without recourse to Westminster?

There are one or two small lobster boats inshore and further
out a yacht with magnificent white sails, catching the best of
the day as it sweeps northwards. It is hard to believe that more
than a thousand years ago people also sailed these waters, in the
smallest and flimsiest of craft – could a coracle really have
brought Columba from Ireland? Ireland may be but 17 miles
distant from Kintyre and Islay, but it would need a superhuman
confidence or a steadfast belief in divine protection to entrust
your being to those waters in such a thing.

Secure, well-surfaced and direct roads are a 20th-century

phenomenon in the West and North of Scotland – for all of our history up until comparatively recently travel by sea was the easiest and best way. These Western Isles are also know in Gaelic as 'the islands of the stranger' – the strangers being the sea-going Vikings who invaded, captured and colonised the area from the eighth century onwards, and did it all by galley (even to the extent of marking out and claiming territory by having one drawn across the isthmus of Tarbert in Kintyre). They sacked precious and sacred Iona in 794, destroying even the library and within 50 years they were rulers of the entire northern and western seaboard, as far south as the Isle of Man.

For over four centuries it was the Vikings who were the masters of this part of Scotland – and their influence can still be felt. Not only are there excavated settlements – Udal in North Uist is one of the largest – but many of the place names have Norse roots. Dispute and fighting were their way of life (later with each other rather than the remnants of the original population) but as they settled, interbred and grew established they added their contribution to the culture we now know. What we regard as pure Gaelic – in history and origin – is often nothing of the sort but an admixture of Gael and Gall: the type of admixture that has made the name MacLeod one of the most common of island names yet one that springs directly from the settling of a relative of the Norse King of Man called Liotr at Dunvegan, to guard the Minch and administer the Norse dominions.

Order has been kept here by the exercise of naval power for all of the succeeding centuries. And where national order has broken down, it has been because the local chiefs have been stronger and had more boats and men to harry, to pillage and to impose discipline. The Lord of the Isles is a title that is now subsumed amongst the many that hang like Christmas decorations on Prince Charles. It once meant something here, because the title was taken by force and maintained by sea power.

Indeed there was a sentimental attachment to the title even in this century: there was much muttering and criticism when Lord Leverhulme – soap merchant extraordinary and owner of Lewis and then Harris, which he tried to 'improve' only to ground on the rock of local resistance – took the title Viscount Leverhulme of the Western Isles. It seemed too close to the real thing to be acceptable.

As we cross in the lee of Skye towards North Uist which is becoming more and more defined on the horizon I recall that one traveller this century – in the same year as Muir was traversing Scotland – ended his journey at this spot, in sight of the Western Isles, but was beaten back by the weather. Sir Alastair Dunnett was one of the 'Canoe Boys', the other being the redoubtable Seumas Adam. In the early part of the 1930s Dunnett and Adam – with an enthusiasm for all things Scottish – started an adventure magazine for boys called *The Claymore*. When it ran out of money they were left with a hefty printer's bill to pay and no apparent means of meeting it. With the spirit of their magazine in mind – a spirit that imbued both of them – they resolved to pay off their debts by canoeing from the Clyde to the Hebrides, making money by writing despatches for the *Daily Record* along the way. It was a madcap scheme, during which they nearly lost their canoes and their lives on a number of occasions, but they made it as far as Dunvegan until the autumn weather broke and they had to 'make another move forward as clearly as we could see – one day we simply packed up our logs and charts and the trip was over.'

Dunnett subsequently had his record of the journey published in 1950 as *Quest by Canoe* and this was re-issued by NWP in 1995 this time more fittingly as, *The Canoe Boys*. At the end of the book Dunnett attempted to address the age-old 'Highland Problem' and suggests a solution:

'Sincere men and committees', he wrote, 'have been publishing reports and recommendations for 200 years. There was one common flaw in these plans. None of them conceded that Scotland, as a nation and an economic unit, must be the whole basis of the solution.

'Our solutions are of a simple if whole-hearted character.

First the planning must be conceived and done from Scotland, although the lack of such an authority should not delay their starting...The key solution to the Highland problem is transport and communications. After that comes the use of the land and its assets, for the first time in a modern and efficient setting. That is the whole story.'

When his book was first published in 1950, Dunnett still believed in such a solution – though it had not yet come about. But a start had been made on it, and Dunnett was closer to that than most, for he spent the war years as press officer to Secretary of State Tom Johnston, before becoming editor of the *Daily Record* in 1946 and of The *Scotsman* in 1956. He continued to espouse the principal of Scottish control of Scottish issues – of devolution – when that subject was off the political agenda for most of the immediate post-war years.

Until he recently passed away he openly supported independence, seeing it as the logical extension of the need for Scottish solutions to the issues and circumstances he discovered in 1934. I recall with affection talking to him on the phone, seeking his wise counsel about problems and getting clear, calm advice. In 1997 he and Seumas Adam belatedly received the annual award of the *Scots Independent* newspaper for those who have contributed most to Scottish life and letters, and I spoke at the awards' lunch – grateful at last to have met two such visionary Scots.

There is still a slight swell from the earlier bad weather, and although it is summer there is a cold breeze coming across from the islands. After a turn around the decks I go down to sit in the bar, and meet two people I knew in Uist 15 years ago when I lived there. There is a particular Western Isles phrase – 'Are you home for a few days' – that greets visitors who are connected in some way to the community. I am glad to hear it from them: as glad as I was the first time I heard it asked of me. It means, to me at least, that others know that this place is as much home now as anywhere, save a small part of Argyll.

We catch up on what we have all being doing. They know my story without me telling it, so it gets discounted with a brief bit of humour about seeing me more often these days then they did when I lived on Benbecula. (It is the same thing I get in Glendaruel – perhaps put a bit more kindly than the Glen farmer who told me to my face that he wasn't coming to a village ceilidh I had been asked to chair, because he was damned if he was going to pay to hear me, when he could hear me for free on his television even though he didn't want to!) They both work in the council offices and have been on the mainland on a course. They are cynical about working for the local authority – Comhairle Nan Eilean – believing that the reputation of council workers has reached rock bottom.

One of them says, 'It'll just get worse with this parliament of yours. We'll be left as usual with the rubbish to do, and no money to do it. We thought things couldn't get worse after the Tories – but they have. And they'll get worse still.'

I am about to argue but get stopped in my tracks by the other one: 'Don't get us wrong,' he interjects, 'I've voted SNP for the last twenty years, and I want the parliament and more. But you'll have to go some to persuade any of us that it is going to undo the damage we've seen done to the councils we've worked in. Where's the money going to come from, for a start? And where are the good people going to come from, people not just to stand – though we could do with more of those instead of some of the numpties we get – but also to work? I wouldn't advise anyone to follow what I have done.'

The bar of a CalMac ferry doesn't seem the place to start an exposition of Scotland's wealth, and the subsidy we've been paying south of the border for the last 20 years. In any case that argument seems, in a curious way, to have been proved and disproved: proved because it is true and most people accept it as true, disproved because there is a stronger feeling that government today cannot do the things it wants to no matter the resources available to it.

So there is a gap between expectation and actuality: most people expect government to spend more on society's needs, but equally most people don't think the money is there to spend. Perhaps this is a result of distant politics for too long –

perhaps the residue of 18 years of Conservatism that knew the price of everything and the value of nothing. And perhaps it reflects the consumerism of our age – the aspiration to possess more and more material goods, with the knowledge that most people will never have enough to afford them all.

We get off politics eventually, and onto island matters. Work has started on the new £6.6m causeway to Berneray, that will provide a permanent link for the island to North Uist and thus to Benbecula and the south. There are rumours of further job losses at the MOD rocket range – and so it goes on. Places feel like home for a variety of reasons – including the fact that you know the names and faces of those that are talked about in gossip, and you understand the concerns with things that seem trivial in other settings. And they feel like home because each corner, each view is associated with other moments of passing or viewing.

I go back up on deck to watch the boat come in through the 'maddies' – the rocks that guard the entrance to Lochmaddy and are so called from the Gaelic 'madadh' meaning dog (with a wild connotation), or a wolf. There are a group of young Germans on deck, with motorbikes, exploring the Celtic world that they know from Runrig and a dozen other bands. They have been noisy on the way over, but they are silent now as the length of the loch opens up (it covers nine square miles, but there are so many bays and inlets that it is alleged its coastline runs for 200 miles) and there is a still sunlight on the edges of the hills. Its beauty is magical, almost otherworldly.

I spent two calm autumn days in Uist last November, promoting my book on the 1930's photographer and film maker, Werner Kissling. Although we left late from Lochboisdale because of an overnight storm, the rest of the time there was an autumnal stillness; a period of calm at that time of year is unusual. Magnificent as the Western Isles can look in a full force 10 gale; it is also decidedly uncomfortable. The house shakes (literally in the case of a caravan I stayed in for my wild first winter in Benbecula in 1977; the walls used to bulge visibly as I lay in bed, listening to the storm), driving becomes risky and walking impossible. Such storms also mean not just disruption of transport but no deliveries of milk or fresh vegetables – although now with a bakery on Benbecula, at least bread is available.

And if visibility falls then the plane doesn't come either, so there are no papers, there is no mail and people can spend two or three days waiting to leave or camping out in Glasgow waiting to come home.

Many people who work for the council, or the Hydro or any number of other organisations must also give up their schedule. That might mean a visit to Barra for a day, or Eriskay for an afternoon. The new causeway to Berneray will mean much more than just easy access – it will mean a security of visits from a doctor or a health visitor, and no regular winter interruptions to the visits of the itinerant music or art teacher. Doubtless the rabbit population of North Uist will also use it to colonise Berneray. And because the ferry will no longer run, and the causeway will not be tolled, it will make life a little cheaper for those who live there or who have to visit: transport progress that Skye can only envy!

Coming off the Uig ferry I metaphorically tip my hat at the Bank of Scotland branch in Lochmaddy and the manager's house that sits by it – they *have* been a 'friend for life', and a constant help in managing my sometime chaotic finances. They are all the proof I need that a long-standing relationship with one's bank (and a predilection to admit to the truth rather than try to hide it) is the best way to ensure satisfaction on both sides!

My purpose for visiting Uist in this journey is, however, not simply the pleasure of the pilgrimage. With Muir in mind I want to look at the definable changes in one part of this island group since 1934. By co-incidence it is a subject I have studied lately and I want to refresh my memory and talk to one or two people to see if there is another view of Scotland in that year to set alongside Muir's. I drive down through North Uist and Benbecula, resisting the temptation to stop here or there to talk to people I know and have not seen for some time. I do detour through Balivanich, now a positive metropolis for the islands, though in Muir's time it was a tiny township by the sea.

The principal airfield for the island was established here before the war (there had been other airstrips – for example at Sollas in North Uist) and around it grew a military presence of sorts. But it was only in 1956 that the Government decided to establish a rocket-testing range on neighbouring South Uist, and placed the administrative HQ here on Benbecula. It formed the focus for further development, army housing and then the offices of the new single-tier authority for the Western Isles that was formed in 1974. Then came the bank, the health board offices, an upgrading of the barracks, an upgrading of the school and a new airport building – now it sprawls in all directions, and sticks out like a very sore, white and damp streaked thumb on the flat machair land.

But like ancient Italian cities, it seems to start suddenly (country one minute, buildings the next) and finish as abruptly. There are a row of squaddies' houses (in one of which my wife lived for a year with two other young primary teachers) and then a hardware shop and nothing – back to the sprinkling of new croft houses on the island landscape. One has to look in the mirror to make sure it was not a rather tacky mirage.

Another 15 minutes and I am well past the remarkable new secondary school at Liniclete – an outstandingly successful piece of design and planning – past the Creagorry Hotel where I have spent many a happy hour, and across the South Ford and into South Uist. Somewhere embedded in the wall of the causeway that sweeps across the Ford is a 150lb rock that demolished my house at Kilerevagh on an April evening in 1983, making Cathleen and I homeless and virtually without possessions. A blasting 'mistake' made the face of the temporary quarry a quarter of a mile away shoot up and out, rather than down and in, and propelled this geological missile through our roof, past my wife (who was watering a New Zealand begonia...that statement looked odd in the police report) and into the foundations, by way of a comfy chair I was about to sit down on to watch the six o'clock news. The contractors admitted liability to my solicitor the next day with the memorable phrase 'Well, it wisnae a fucking great seagull that dropped it, was it?'

I detour again round Iochdar, one of my favourite communities in Uist, a painting of which still dominates my lounge in Argyll. The old black house where Penny Bheagh lived – she was one of the great traditional singers of her time – is a ruin but the old schoolhouse opposite looks as if it is inhabited. I slow down in a passing place, and a car pulls in alongside me: we are about to give the all purpose Uist wave when I recognise one of the teachers at the local school: we wind windows down and chat about the weather, our families, the state of the old buildings and a dozen other things. Not a car comes to hoot at us and move us on – we are blocking the road – and the pace of life seems about right for human interaction.

This road leads to Ardivachar, and one of the most westerly tips of the UK: the copy of the Doomsday book given to the USA for its bicentenary celebrations is mounted on Ardivachar granite, not just ancient rock, but rock with a modern significance, as this point was the first part of the country seen by lend-lease pilots, flying their planes to Britain during the war. There is a cemetery here, and further along a hut used by the army as part of their patrolling to keep the beach and sea area clear during missile test firings: it is on the edge of the rocket range.

There is a soldier here today, though whether he is on duty or just skiving it is hard to tell. He certainly doesn't look alert and ready to repel an imminent invasion. It is surprisingly difficult to engage in casual conversation the only other person within sight, but I saunter up to him and remark on the weather. He grunts, but eventually starts to chat. He is from England, and has been posted here for the last year. 'I thought I'd hate it' he says. 'It's miles from anywhere and I was in Germany before this – you could have a night in Hamburg and really live. Here having a pint is a big deal.' But he has begun to discover things he likes. 'It's not that I like the quiet life – I don't. That's not what I joined the army for. 'But here', he gestures to the hills to the south and to the sea in front, 'there is something special – something that if you just stand and look you begin to feel what it is to be alive and in the world.'

His introspection worries him. 'Sometimes I just come out here for a walk – there's nothing doing today – there's no units in. And I wonder why I am doing it, and what I should be doing with the rest of my life.' He's not married – he is only 24 – but he is on a voyage of discovery. 'I joined up because I didn't have a job, and I had no chance – I mean no chance – of getting one. And I like the army and the mates I have. But maybe there is more to it – and maybe I can find out what that is.'

He hasn't been anywhere else in Scotland, and doesn't really want to see the rest of it. 'There's too many Jocks in the army,' he says with half a laugh. 'No offence, but I don't need to meet any more and see where they live. And I don't really understand the people here – some speak in a funny language, and the ones that work with us don't seem all there. But they've got a great place, although I don't think they know it – and the weather can be shit.'

I ask him about the parliament and if anyone has spoken to him about it – but he only knows the vaguest details and seems to see it as a bit of an affront to him and his mates: 'If you want to bugger off on your own, then do it. We'll just be able to stop paying for you – more for us!' Yet he is not hostile, nor even, one might say, concerned. Maybe the Uist machair and the hills have taken the edge off him today. We stand and smoke and I tell him I made a film about the range some years ago. He seems keen to talk about the missiles and what has been fired here, and what he would like to fire. He is doubtful about the future of the place – 'costs too much and not enough people use it' – but would like to stay for a while. Suddenly he looks at his watch, and says he had better be off – not, as I first think because there is some inflexible military event to be attended to, but because there will be tea served back at the base in half an hour. He ambles up the beach and I turn back to my car. Within minutes there is no one at all in sight.

I take the road back round to join the main north/south highway which is gradually being improved and made into a double track. And I drive on, as they say here, 'up south' to the Lochboisdale Hotel where I am meeting someone from Eriskay. Werner Kissling stayed every year in the Lochboisdale Hotel and I have grown to like it too. It doesn't have a phone, a trouser press and a mini bar in every bedroom, but it does have huge baths and beds that give a good night's sleep. I sit in the public bar and listen to stories of the island of Eriskay in 1934. I can see them in my mind's eye, because the first film that used Gaelic was made there in that year, by the enigmatic Kissling – soldier, diplomat, scholar, gentleman, as his gravestone in Dumfries records, though it has missed out 'photographer and film maker', and these latter were his greatest talents.

While Muir was bemoaning the state of the Glasgow slums, and the dereliction of Lanarkshire, Eriskay was a community that had changed little since the late 19th century. It didn't have running water either, and the wells were not in the most convenient places. But the traditional strengths of the community – communal work, a spread of activities that gave different support at different times of the year, a Catholic solidarity that virtually embraced everyone on the island – made the place operate effectively and created a sense of valuable belonging and interdependence.

It was, I suppose, in that basis like Muir's Orkney – although Orkney was much more wealthy ('moderately prosperous' according to Muir, but that is in comparison to the mainland, not to the Western Isles) and its agricultural methods much more advanced. Muir called the farms 'very pleasant, easily worked and profitable places', and puts this down to 'science' although he does not define that word. Its similarity lay in the fact that life there was 'humanly desirable and good', though also 'quite eccentric to the economic life of modern civilisation'. Life in Eriskay was harder, but it also retained its virtues because of – as in Muir's Orkney – 'a happy series of drawbacks, or what seem at first sight to be drawbacks: by its isolation for centuries from the rest of Scotland and Great Britain, an isolation which has enabled it to preserve its traditional ways of life, so that until today it has scarcely been touched by the competitive spirit of Industrialisation'.

And Eriskay had an additional drawback that was also a strength – its retention of Gaelic as the principal (virtually only in 1934) language of the islanders, a language that was in steep decline elsewhere, and had been since the 15th century. My Eriskay friend is less hopeful about the present and past. Admittedly the population decline of the 60s and 70s has been stopped – the population is presently rising slightly, and there is piped water, electricity, television and even a pub.

But the ferry service – dependent as it still is on the tidal conditions of the sound, which virtually dries out between each high tide – is not reliable enough. A causeway, such as the one to Berneray, is the answer but funding for it is still at the far end of the pipeline. 'If we can have our causeway, then people can live on Eriskay, but still work here in Uist. The car ferry helps, but it is not the answer. It's only the start of the answer.'

And there are less tangible, but equally pressing problems. 'There's no real solidarity left', he says. 'Oh, you might get someone to help you one day, but go for a ceilidh and the television is on – where are the stories that my father used to tell, or the songs my mother sang.'

'Why don't you tell them', I suggest.

'I do from time to time, but the youngsters aren't interested and the older folk have got out of the way of sitting and listening and taking part. An evening in the hall, or down at the pub, is the way we see others living their lives, and we live our life that way too.'

I remind him of something that Kissling wrote at the end of his life:

I have had the good fortune to live with the people of the Western Isles a good many years ago, before the most important changes affecting the rural scene had taken place and so be able to record the old ways. Everywhere today the new houses are being built to uniform specifications: the black house has disappeared – not necessarily a matter for regret – but with it has disappeared many a ceilidh and by degrees the desire for spontaneous self-expression by the people, be it in song and poetry, the making of tools or the dyeing of home-made tweeds. Can they – or can we – do without it?

There is along pause, filled by the sound of the juke box. 'No', says my friend, 'we can't do without it, and yet it has gone.'

There is a longer pause. Someone is shouting out the back – drink has been taken.

'No', he says again, 'but maybe we can make something new if we want to. Maybe we can make Gaelic live, and teach the songs, and make new ones, and remember what we had. Maybe – but probably not.'

Yet instead of staring down and thinking, he smiles suddenly.

'I'll tell you what we have done', he remarks. 'We have done what we wanted to do – we have made Eriskay part of the modern world – a place you can get to in a day from London or Edinburgh, and a place where you can sit in your kitchen and watch television and drink tea and read the day's newspaper and phone your cousin in America and go to the freezer and take out a burger. That's what I wanted to do when I was young, and we've done it. So maybe I'm wrong: it's just the way of the world and we have what we set out to get.'

He seems much more cheerful after that. And he gets enthusiastic about what the children on Eriskay today will be able to do: work from home on the Internet and still keep the croft: drive to Uist on the causeway for a drink in the evening and still go home to their families.

'God', he says, 'they might even want to be in that

parliament you keep going on about. And that parliament might hear about Eriskay and discover it wasn't such a backward place as they thought. In fact, if it goes on like this, it might be the parliament that was backward – Eriskay is on the cutting edge!'

Next morning on the boat to Oban I have the slight dim ache of an incipient hangover. I have had a Hebridean evening, of the best sort. Conversation, drink and more conversation. Moments of depression at what has happened, and moments of elation at what lies before. Laughter and even a little song, though it was little and late and not necessarily well received by the players at the pool table.

Now I am going from my would-be, once-was, home to my real home. To another type of Highland life, whose roots sometimes seem even less well planted than those that lie in the wake of this (modern) ferry to the isles. But which, like everywhere I have been, is consciously or unconsciously 'in waiting' for its future.

Chapter Eleven
Argyll

Argyll is a vast county – or Argyll and Bute is, for that is its formal name (and one must not forget the little island of Bute at the south of the county). It covers the second largest area of any local authority in Scotland – 40 times larger than wee Clackmannan, although it has only double the population. Its southernmost point – at the tip of the Mull of Kintyre – is geographically further south than towns and villages in Northumberland in England! To the north it runs to within a few miles of Fort William.

Its shoreline is so indented that it covers almost 2000 miles, and the county contains no less than 90 islands ranging from the expanse of Mull to rocky outcrops that contain a few seals and sheep. It probably has thousands of sea rocks and islets. The largest town in Argyll is still Dunoon, although Oban has grown fast and will probably outstrip it eventually. But neither of these is the county town – that honour belongs to Lochgilphead, which supplanted Inveraray at the local government reorganisation in 1975 and which now houses the administration of the area at the grandly named Kilmory Castle.

Argyll as a county is run by a motley group of independent councillors (all claiming to be non-political) who have been forged into a pseudo-political group by a Dunoon councillor with an inordinate amount of ambition. Like most marriages of convenience the cracks started to show as soon as it was consummated and a divorce is imminently expected – precipitated most probably by the electoral expulsion of most of those who took part in this foolish and failed experiment in local governance. Independent in name only, it has veered from side to side at the whim of pork barrel politics and obscure local vendettas providing poorer and poorer services and more and more controversy.

In parliamentary terms the constituency (which is smaller than the administrative county and excludes Helensburgh and parts of Loch Lomond) has been equally fickle in its choices, having been represented since 1974 by three different parties. Only Labour has failed to get a look in.

But there is more to life than politics! Argyll is a county with great diversity which faces the Firth of Clyde but has most of its body in the Highlands. It is Gaelic in spirit, but the language has all but died out except in the furthermost islands, and because it does not lie on the way to anywhere of importance – by that I mean anywhere that is on the way up in population or influence – it is less visited, and has retained more of its original character. The north of the county I know a little, largely because of travelling from the ferry port of Oban to Glasgow and Edinburgh when I lived in the Western Isles. Then I was prepared to undertake the five- or eight-hour boat trip (five hours direct from Lochboisdale, eight if you came via Barra, and the choice was Caledonian MacBrayne's, not yours) before a three- or four-hour drive.

It is easiest to fly to Uist – an hour from Glasgow will get you to Benbecula for as long as the airport is there: recently it has fallen prey to erosion as the west coast of the islands does from time to time. Otherwise you can drive to Uig on Skye, as I did from Inverness, taking perhaps six hours from the central belt, and then sail for two hours or so to Lochmaddy. However, the shorter car journey to Oban carries the penalty of a longer boat trip – fine in the summer in good weather, but not so good when there is a force eight blowing. I have even crossed the Minch at this widest part in a force 10, gusting to force 11: life jackets were broken out at one stage, and the boat listed into Castlebay where lorries were literally crowbarred apart after the battering of the storm.

The extreme west I do not know at all – I have been to Campbeltown once, in my first year out of university, working as a Church of Scotland bureaucrat sent to talk to a dismal and dreary church congregation. On the way back I had to call with a colleague at a church hostel for recovering alcoholics in an old country house on the Mull of Kintyre, facing the sea. We sat at Formica-topped tables in the echoing dining room and I felt the frustration and hopelessness of a dozen men whose decline was measured by the fact that they were prepared now to trust this place, rather than themselves with the whole of any future they had.

I have lived in Cowal – described in the *Encyclopaedia of Scotland* 'the south-eastern extremity of Argyll between the sea lochs Long and Fyne' – for most of the 90s and hope to live here for a lot longer – because I have found the place I want to stay. I have written this book sitting at my desk looking out across Loch Riddon to the hills above the Kyles of Bute. My garden in front of the house has suffered from my penance at the word processor, but as the months have passed the roses I am training up a new arch have thickened and the first flowers (three years after planting) have opened, large and heavy and a delicate yellow, but with far less scent than the old, deep, scarlet rose that flowers in profusion by the door.

This house was built sometime around 1790, but the place is recorded on a 16th-century map, and if I crane my neck a little I can see nearby the ruin of one of the older buildings behind which I have hidden my central heating oil tank! The name *Feorlean* means, in its proper non-anglicised spelling, a 'farthing' in the old sense of a measurement of land. But collo-quially in Gaelic it also means a 'meadow between two hills'. The description fits. On one side the hill rises up, across our boundary (which is the line of the forestry plantation) and then goes on, splitting into two peaks which can get a touch of snow in the winter while we down here are being rained upon. On the other there is a more modest crag, giving a sheer rock-face edge to the small formal garden, sloping down to the track that winds up from the main road.

This shelter makes the spot fertile and warm – we can sit on the patio that runs almost the full length of the whitewashed traditional farmhouse and complain of the heat, whilst the tops of the trees bend in a half-gale. We are only open to the storms from the north-east, where a funnel in the hills intensifies the cold blast, knocking panes out of the greenhouse and shaking the skylight in the bedroom. In the summer, with the trees in full leaf, I cannot see another house from where I sit now. In the winter I can glimpse through the branches (and through the bare azalea that produces a blizzard of scented yellow in the spring) the 19th-century whitewashed mock baronial pile of Ormidale House, and its pier where one of Neil Munro's 'Para Handy' stories starts.

The only sign that other human beings are in the world is the rising line a good way up the hill on the other side of the loch marking the new road to Tighnabruaich. At night the headlights sparkle briefly as they turn the top corner, and then descend like fireflies until hidden by a cutting a half-mile from the top. On frosty nights the winking orange warning light of the slow-moving gritter on this road reminds us to go out and cover any fragile plants.

We bought the house in 1992, when Cathleen became the head teacher of the local school in Glendaruel and since then have spent all the money we don't have on restoring it. This is 'Phase One', as we call it, of a plan which will probably never be completed, but which has already seen the gutting of every room, the installing of a bright red stove in the kitchen that gives us hot water, cooking and central heating, and has also brought into human use for the first time in two centuries the byre which is now serves as our wood-floored lounge and extra sleeping space.

As I write this the loch is filling up, the tide coming to full, and today it is black and limpid, with a touch of silver on the edges where the shore slopes up and where the river channel runs through. There is a grey sky, and the midges are enjoying the wettest summer in a generation: I have closed the study window to stop myself being eaten alive.

On the desk beside me my well-thumbed copy of *Scottish Journey* lies open at the place where Muir describes his 'down the watter' trip to Campbeltown, Muir was somewhat astonished that he could leave the grime of Glasgow and find himself so quickly in rural, Highland Scotland. 'One can feel the enchantment of the Highlands', he says, 'by taking a few steps out of Glasgow to the north or the north-west; and that seems at first one of the strangest things about it. The natural explanation', he adds, 'is that Glasgow is only the extreme fringe of a whole sea of grime and dirt extending eastwards almost to within sight of Edinburgh. To the north-west of Glasgow the sea washes against the hills and in between them until it is spent.'

This explanation, natural or not, seems simplistic. I am no fonder of the relics of industrialisation than he was of their more immediate effects, but there is no 'sea of grime' – failures of course, and spectacularly unpleasant ones at that. But Argyll and Cowal are different from Glasgow because they have different roots and different causes for their present condition. The sea is only one of them.

Muir described the Clyde resorts of Argyll as 'honest towns of pleasure where the holiday maker is expected to pay, but where he gets something substantial in return: the quantity of entertainment in such places as Dunoon and Rothesay is unstinted.' Today such resorts are a shadow of their former selves; the crowds which virtually swamped the piers on hot July days at the turn of the century are now a matter of history. During a recent Glasgow holiday weekend the paddle steamer *Waverley* was actually out of service for essential maintenance, such was the conviction of her owners that no great commercial loss would be felt. Times have truly changed on the Clyde.

It is the airports that are swamped now, whilst Dunoon

and Rothesay and a score of other towns on the Clyde coast endlessly try to re-invent themselves to achieve levels of prosperity which are but memories. For almost 30 years that was not even attempted in Dunoon, basking as it was in the easy dollars of American sailors who worked on the sinister depot ships in the Holy Loch. Then, after the collapse of the USSR and the Berlin Wall, the bubble of war in the northern hemisphere burst and the 'peace dividend' for the town was potential impoverishment.

It has reacted to the change pretty well. The local economy, while not tremendously robust, has adapted to the needs of Glasgow commuters (the ferry service still permits that) and to the skimming past of endless bus tours, packed with old-age pensioners from Burnley, Bradford and similar places. Against strong and long-standing resistance the town centre has been cosmetically made-over and parking has been restricted, making easy access more difficult, but with little discernible effect on local trade. A more radical plan to impose parking charges – hardly necessary, at least in the way in which they are meant to deter car use – has been quietly shelved by the council, as they have enough reasons to be considered unpopular without inventing any more.

Dunoon being my nearest town of any size (25 minutes away on a single-track road), I shop there from time to time. We have lived in the area long enough to know that Cathleen or I will always meet people we know in the street or the supermarket. But the place I know best, which I use as my political thermometer, is the community in which I live. Agatha Christie's Miss Marple solved her crimes by making comparisons with the life of her village of St Mary Mead. Mired as I sometimes am in journalists' views (often worse informed than their readers would dare suspect), in focus groups and in the breadth of opinion and gossip of a political party, there is something refreshing in consulting those about whom one knows the minutiae as well as the broad brush strokes: whom one can place in their whole context and therefore weigh their views against their lives. It is a useful, melodious and often meaningful counterpoint to the political dissonance all around.

Consultation, of course, is too formal a word. Conversation would be a better one – conversations that can take place in the bar of the Colintraive Hotel, in a house overlooking the loch, in a passing place as we go in different directions, or round my kitchen table as another bottle is produced. If one thinks about these conversations, reflects upon them and assesses them over a period of time it is possible to get a snapshot (no more or less) of a whole range of issues facing people in their lives, and where they interface with their hopes and desires. To assess, in short, if there is anything for which they are 'in waiting' and what that thing might be.

Some incidents in the last year:

An English friend tells me that he might vote SNP at the next election. He can't see why Scotland can't do better than it does and all he has heard from New Labour is excuses.

A colleague of Cathleen's expresses doubts about Scotland because the whole country seems to be too 'anti' everything.

Two guests talk about a 'sense of excitement' after the referendum and want the new parliament to be a fresh start. They particularly want the parliament to do something about rural housing and the fact that young people in this community have to leave because they cannot afford to buy a house anywhere.

A public meeting about a plan for a new ferry mooring expresses its anger at being talked down to and taken for granted by Caledonian MacBrayne. The community wants to be consulted, not ignored.

Despite the efforts of a couple of individuals, there seems a general apathy about getting a community transport scheme off the ground – no one thinks anything can change. But there is a community push on to upgrade the village hall.

The suggested closure of the local school meets a wall of opposition. A sustained campaign has to rely on half a dozen activists, yet it succeeds.

Another school closure (my wife's this time) goes through by underhand means: there is fury locally but as the weeks pass nobody does anything about it.

If I had the discipline to keep a diary I would have dozens more pointers to what is happening here: on the one hand a growing self-confidence and self-assertion: on the other a stagnation and apathy which leaves opportunities not taken because there is no hope of things being any different in the future.

And both of these symptoms are apparent at the same time. Or rather both in the same place – with some people flexing their muscles and devoting their time and energy to change, whilst others with no desire to get involved who live their lives with perhaps only a glance back at the world as it passes, remain defensive.

Nothing new in that. But perhaps there has been a subtle shift. Some of those in the disinterested camp have moved a little towards enthusiasm. And there has been no movement the other way. Not exactly a revolution, or even the stirrings of fully-fledged evolution, but enough of a difference to make me think that *something is happening*. If it is happening here amongst the grass roots of a rural continuity and against the background noise of economic and social decline, then perhaps it is happening elsewhere more strongly, and with more visible effect.

It could be argued that rural continuity (by which I mean

the actual impact of the seasons, and the proximity to the soil and the fruits of the sea which is the way of life as well as the means of earning a living for so many here) coupled with social and economic decline should force the pace, not slow it down. But you can only render people so many knocks before they become wary. And wariness is a rural characteristic – in its best Highland sense it means self-confidence and an inner contentment and certainty: in its worse it is a protection against intrusion of any sort.

If Muir had driven through this glen in 1934 he would have found a very different place. For a start there was not one school with nine pupils, but three schools and a total school population of over fifty. There were two shops (not one part-time sub-post office, though it is a good one, organised with energy) two hotels and a tea room, two churches and a healthy farming population as well as a regular influx of tourists during the summer. The agricultural depression (which almost mirrored the industrial depression in its intensity and length) had certainly taken its toll, but the farms were still operating and men were still employed on them in addition to the farmer's family.

The population had of course declined from the 19th century but it was about to rise again, as forestry became an important industry. New houses for the forestry workers were built after the war and many people settled here and elsewhere throughout Scotland, away from the cities. Road transport was more difficult (the new road to Tighnabruaich was only built in the 60s), but transport by boat was then something more than a novelty. The puffers did pass the loch and stop at Ormidale Pier, and the steamers did call there and at Colintraive.

During the Second World War the loch was used to house 'gunpowder ships' – floating storage for ammunition located away from the population centre of Scotland in case of attack or accident. The navy took over Caladh Castle on the other side of the loch, reducing it over a few short years to a ruin which was blown up afterwards. Now there are trees and briars where the grand house once stood, and a three-mile winding track to the home farm (bought by a German businessman who lives there part of the time) and to the whitewashed cottage were the local SNP councillor Sandy MacQueen lives with his wife Carol, seven dogs and lots of ducks. It is easier to get to them by boat, and in the summer one of the best ways of spending a day is to wait for them at the green boathouse on this side of the loch, and then putter out in the wee *Kirsty Stewart* (a beautifully restored small wooden boat, named after their first grandchild), bound for a bay on Bute with a picnic and a drink at Colintraive on the way home.

The great houses are the most obvious casualties of the last 50 years. Near Maymore Farm (where we lived for three months when we first came here) the entrance to the old estate of the glen is marked by an ornamental gateway, a reproduction of the gate to the city of Lucknow in India. It was erected by Sir Colin Campbell, the hero who lifted the siege of Lucknow during the Indian Mutiny, and whose home was here – a home he married into, becoming the proprietor of the glen by that fortunate alliance.

But the big house is long gone – this time the victim of a fire which ended a long decline from family home to increasingly seedy hotel. The site is now occupied by a caravan park – well run and attractively laid out and probably the biggest attraction in the place. Dunans Castle at the head of the glen is still standing, but the Fletcher family who occupied it for years has gone, and it has been bought by some unknown who hopefully will have the money to restore its massive leaking roof and decaying rooms.

I do not regret the passing of the feudal structure in places such as this, but it has to be acknowledged that egalitarianism by accident has its price. The focus for employment has gone and with it a fragmentation of opportunity: nothing is big enough to provide both employment and tied housing and nothing has been created to secure those things.

If one of the pillars of the social and economic structure falls, then the others may not be strong enough to hold it up. Not even the church (a beautiful 17th-century church in the glen guarding an even older graveyard) serving the two parishes of Kilmodan and Colintraive with one minister, nor the local culture which was Gaelic even at the turn of the century (Gaelic place names abound and in my house there was some knowledge of Gaelic until the Second World War) and which now aspires to Highland virtues while being leavened with southern Scots like me and others from even further away, can do that. It is the fallen pillars of the traditional order in such places which give cause for concern – for if there is no structure, then there can be no re-building. However, it may be that new pillars are being formed.

I have never lived in a place that was so concerned with local democracy. By that I do not mean that there is an endless ferment of electioneering – elections are quiet enough things here, with little of the razzmatazz which is becoming prevalent elsewhere. But there is a keen sense that the powers of government – particularly local government – are important and that the area is not being served well by present arrangements. Its councillors are part of that movement of criticism and change – on one side of the loch is Sandy, and on my side Robert MacIntyre, who has recently left the ranks of the independents to join the SNP.

They are energetic and committed – they are known to almost everyone and they are a first port of call with problems, not a final solution. They are full of ambition for their areas, and for Argyll as a whole and they not only listen and attempt to act, but they also propose and suggest. I am not saying that this is a phenomenon unique to SNP councillors. Locally there are good and energetic Liberals and a Labour councillor in Dunoon, but it is a characteristic not found in the independent group – mostly community mavericks with little vision. It seems that here in Argyll there is a move to make things better than they are, and that that move is tied up with a belief in self-help, in the community as a starting point, harnessing to it the powers that exist within the council.

That same energy is beginning – just beginning – to show itself in concerns for what the Scottish Parliament can do. The local paper – which eschews politics most of the time in favour of the pressure of advertisements – has begun to fill up with stories of local maladministration, of candidate selection and of problems that need to be addressed. And fill up editorially, and on the letters pages, always the safety valve for the politically constipated.

The old pillars accepted the political establishment as it was. As the pillars decayed some political freedom asserted itself – there was an SNP member here in the 70s and John MacKay – the Tory who took over in 1979 – did not last very long. The Highland Liberal tradition was re-asserted with the election of Ray Michie, who is personally popular and easy to talk to.

But now that the pillars have crumbled further, there is a need to establish a new order. In a partisan way I want that order to include my own party, but in many senses that is less important than the acceptance of the new order across the political spectrum, in response to what people are actually discovering for themselves. A need, certainly, to be involved and to influence what is happening: a desire to draw closer to themselves the levers of power and to make a difference to their own lives, and a rediscovery of the way that working together helps to solve problems.

Times of great change – watersheds – can be identified only in retrospect. Historians have the tools, not contemporary writers with a bee in their bonnet and a bias in their eye.

But I am foolish enough to suggest that perhaps this is one of those times of great change. If the signs of it can be detected in the weak pulse of a sparsely populated glen off Scotland's beaten track, then it must be (and is) even more detectable where the blood runs stronger and the arteries are wider.

The error in going to seek it is to believe that it is a constant theme, one that will be found in every individual and in every action of every community. Change is more inconsistent than that – it seeps out in different channels, and turns back on itself or dries out, or simply does not flow in some of the many shallow tracks it could take. And detecting it suffers from the error of partiality – on both sides: on the side of those who want it because they see it even where it might not be and on the side of those who oppose it because they do not wish to see it.

As I drove down from Oban on the last stage of my journey I passed through Inveraray, once the county town of Argyll and now clogged with tour buses. Its history is a monument to change and an exemplar of how things can be made new. Neil Munro took one view of that process when he wrote:

> O sad for me Glen Aora
> Where I have friends no more
> For lowly lie the rafters
> And the lintels of the door
> The friends are all departed
> The hearthstones black and cold
> And sturdy grow the nettles
> On the place beloved of old.

But there is another view. This little fishing village was burnt by Montrose in 1644 – then it occupied the ground adjacent to the castle and was little more than the service centre for the great castle of the Duke of Argyll. When the new castle was built, the village was moved and a 'model town' was built, its clerk of works being the precursor of the great Adam dynasty, William Adam. The collective effort of two generations of architects produced the core of the place – including the 'Great Inn' which Johnson found 'not only commodious but magnificent'.

Building continued sporadically. The Episcopal Church was erected in the 1860s. The Parish Church, built 70 years earlier, incorporated two distinct parts – one for Gaelic and one for English services. Scotland's greatest comic writer Neil Munro was born here, and witnessed its early 20th-century decline. The puffers and steamers that used to call here have gone, as has the herring, the mainstay of its economy, which even features on the coat of arms and in the town motto – *May there always be a herring in your net*. It even lost its administrative status in Argyll, having to fall back on the fact that it was the first Royal Burgh in the county. Those, however, who make the decisions for the area, or who are petitioners for such decisions, now pass through the streets – crowded with tourists in the summer – on their way to the centre of local power at Lochgilphead.

Yet Inveraray is far from finished. Those tourists have brought money and the ability to restore the town. It has dug into the well of its history and imaginatively presented itself through the town jail, now one of Scotland' major tourist attractions. It hosts festivals for both small boats and Neil Munro, its award-winning whisky shop bottles its own brands and it even has a floating museum, albeit an unimaginatively named one (arctic penguins being an unfamiliar entity here).

Some might argue it has been 'Brigadooned' – artificially tarted up to attract only those who have neither the wit nor the resources to go and find the real Scotland for themselves. Others might point to the complete absence of Gaelic and traditional culture in the town, and to the debasement of its original, hard-working, fishing roots.

But the pillars that created Inveraray fell away a long time ago. The castle is still there, but it too now attracts tourists and as a centre of power is quite irrelevant. The Gaelic side of the church is now its hall for recreation, book sales and tea and coffee. What Inveraray has had to do is survive, and in so doing it has created a new core community, one which is willing to work hard to keep living there. We can bemoan the changes all we want – the facts are 'chiels that winna ding', and these are the facts that Scotland has to face as it enters the new century.

I am not saying that the same medicine must be applied to other locations in Scotland; it has too much to offer to be transformed into a one-dimensional pleasure park. But if our country can pick itself up and not only adjust to, but build upon the opportunities that it has in the world in the way that

Inveraray has, then things will not be as bad as Muir thought they might be.

Certainly Scotland has stood the risk in this last century of losing its 'population, its spirit, its wealth, industry, art, intellect and innate character', as Muir puts it. But the solution is not to lament their going and then hold a wake for them – nor is it, as Muir rightly observes in his criticism of Nationalism in 1934, to 'live in the middle of industrial capitalism as if (the people) were separated from it...to practise the traditional peasant virtues.' That would be, in Muir's own words, 'certainly futile, for traditional virtues take a long time to mature and cannot be created by a mere desire that they should exist, but only by the specific condition that naturally produces them.'

Muir makes these observations with regard to Orkney, but they are valid enough here. 'Certain conditions', he writes, 'aided by human intelligence, have there, after centuries of hardship, produced something which is natural and inevitable and at the same time humanly desirable. The hope for industrial society is that it, too, will eventually develop in this way; but the result will certainly be very different from the Orkney Islands.'

The rate of historical change in our world is increasing. It is not centuries of hardship that are now producing changes emerging around us, but a collective reaction to the decline that Muir witnessed and recorded and which carried on beyond him. And because we now believe more and more in human intervention rather than the natural process, at last Scotland may be trying to create a society that is 'humanly desirable' – though that society will take different forms in different places.

It will undoubtedly create more Inverarays, capitalising on the market that is available to them. But it will also make more industrial estates, technology parks, science centres and all the paraphernalia of economic re-birth, and it will make more books and more films and more theatre and more music because that is how many individuals and groups of people react to what is taking place around them.

The engine of that growth is fuelled by what we have experienced. But to that rich mixture is now added the means by which we may be able to regulate, supervise and energise that growth, the democratic structure without which this country has been unable to bring to fruition the talents that lie all around.

From Inveraray I drive on around the top of Loch Fyne, longing for the umpteenth time for a ferry across this small stretch of water. Argyll is washed by the sea, as Muir claims, and more than just washed – it is parted and sundered and interrupted. The fingers of the sea lochs turn journeys like this into coastal meanderings up and down the same stretch of water, when one's destination is clearly visible on the other side.

After 30 minutes I am at last on the other side, facing Inveraray – a five-minute boat ride away! The town looks neat and orderly and its white buildings remain visible as I drive on to Strachur and past the famous Creggans Inn, bought by the redoubtable Sir Fitzroy MacLean and his wife in the 1950s and since that time one of the most imaginative small hotels in Scotland, where food is not just a necessary evil, but something to celebrate. Its example has been followed throughout the country.

At Strachur I pick up the road to Dunoon then turn right, and soon I am over the hill and descending into Glendaruel – the glen of the two red spots, some say, suggesting a past battle when the river ran with blood, or perhaps more prosaically indicating even then that bracken in the autumn, golden red as it decays, dominated the hillsides. It is ten miles from Dunans Castle to my house. But the ten miles are so full of familiar sights that by the time I turn the corner at the home farm, I feel as if I am already there. Muir finished his travelling as he was met by his wife Willa and son Gavin at Scapa pier in Orkney. This is where I finish mine, rolling down the wide glen road towards my home.

I have not completed the trip in one attempt as he did – I have cut backwards and forwards out of my journey in order to accommodate my everyday life. But I have the same feeling of completeness that he did – a feeling that I know a bit more about my country than I did when I started out, while acknowledging a feeling that there is still much more to know.

The road cuts through a rocky hillock, and I am soon down on the shore, facing Caladh with the hills of Bute rising like a cork to stop up the bottle of the loch. For once it is sunny, and the light lies across Burnt Island, putting in shadow the yachts that are moored by the old boathouse.

I bump onto the track that winds round the hill to my home. I can hear the dogs barking and the gate is open as I turn the final corner to Feorlean.

Chapter Twelve
Conclusion

The trouble with writing books is that the act of writing – in this case the act of travelling and then writing – comes after you have given your publisher two or three paragraphs that sum up what you think will finally see the light of day.

'How stands the real, everyday Scotland as it waits for its democratic future to be born? What do ordinary Scots men and women – and those who have settled here recently – think, expect and want in the new millennium?' These were the questions that I dashed off in a synopsis of this book some three months before I wrote a word, and seven months before I write these last words. As my journey has unfolded and as I have looked more and more into what Edwin Muir recorded and thought, I have kept those questions in mind. In some places I have had a clear answer to the second part – people want action on land ownership, more and better housing, better transport, rural renewal, a fresh and honest democracy, good schools and hospitals. I have seen the evidence of that need throughout the country and contrasted it with the even greater need that Muir observed. Things have got better, but not quickly enough or completely enough. The means to change has not been there, but now it may be coming into being.

I say 'may' because the first question has proved more

difficult to answer. There has been, in some people that I have talked to and in some places I have been, a sense of excitement and anticipation – a real sense of being 'in waiting' for the first Scottish Parliament since 1707. But elsewhere that parliament has seemed to be, if not an irrelevance, then just another structure and just another part of the power play that seems to substitute for real progress.

It is good for people with their noses to the grindstone of politics – politicians, journalists, political groupies – to get out of their claustrophobic environment for a while and to realise that politics is not at the heart and centre of every life. The effect of politics may touch everyone: the things that are not done, or left undone, and the things that should be done if there was the will to find the money and the courage to implement the solution. But the actual acts of politics are the enthusiasm of the few.

One of the first lessons I have learnt from my journey is that we should try to make politics – from its mundane definition of representative decision taking to its most high flown, as the implementation of vision – more accessible, more interesting, more involving. The responsibility to do so lies not just with politicians, but with journalists and the groupies: and the opportunity is available. If we can construct this new parliament on different principles and if we can give ownership of it not to the political parties but to the people, then we have a chance to engage the attention and energies of our fellow citizens. We have the chance to start to undo – it may be a long process – the negative, dismissive attitude of some who live here and for whom politics has done nothing.

Part of the problem is the disrepute that politicians have brought on themselves. One event does not change perception – but a hammer blow of events, and a catalogue of seeming failure creates a climate that is hard to change. It is no accident that cynicism about the political process grew exponentially in Scotland during the 18 years of Tory government, for that was a government that Scotland did not vote for. But the fact that it has gone on growing in the last year and a half as Labour scandal succeeds Labour scandal and as nothing appears to change, is a cause for worry. People want change but they are beginning not to expect it. *'You are all as bad as each other'* is a phrase I am tired of hearing, but very attentive to each time it does thud on the ears. It is good that the Scottish Parliament will have the strongest code of conduct for its members of any European institution – but more importantly those who enter politics must do so for the right reasons, and must fight to keep those reasons and their beliefs as bright and polished as they can.

Parties should not depress initiative and ambition – they should encourage it. And they should encourage idealism, not scorn it. In one sense it might almost be too late to do so. The dogfight of politics does not interest most people and the road to our new institution is already littered with dogs fighting over scraps of bone. New Labour snarls to defend what it believes it has the right to – the absolute loyalty of the majority of Scots. Helen Liddell on her appointment to the Scottish Office talked of 'serious politics' and there being no place for 'protest votes'. Doesn't she realise that protest is a serious business, and that if people protest, then there is something wrong with what she is offering?

The Tories (in this analogy mangy, thin ageing mongrels now) snap at the heels of the other packs, desperate to stop change and desperate to be considered players in the game. The Liberal Democrats snuffle in the undergrowth, a long way from the action. And my own party – trying to be positive and constructive because only by doing so can we be honest to our vision and our aim – gets distracted by the others, nervous of the attacks, and gets pulled in to the pointless skirmishing. What's more, we often enjoy the scrap.

A politics of ideas and principles – in which we can debate not just the means for us to achieve a better country, but also the ultimate destination of that country – would serve Scotland much better. But all politicians are wary of the bite that may come from nowhere, and are on the defensive, rather than confidently striding forward. Yet these politics of ideas and principles would be more popular and more successful, more inclusive and more attractive, than anything we have now. It would certainly require each and every one of us, from all sides, to give up the perpetual denigration of our opponents and instead accentuate our best case. It would make the job of the rebutters, the dirt diggers and the bruisers redundant and it would need a new lexicon for political journalists, in which 'split', 'bitter', 'gaffe' and 'row' were not present and a new one for politicians, shorn of 'separatist', 'tartan Tory', 'protest vote' – and, yes, shorn of 'betrayal', 'Millbank tendency' and 'phoney Tony' – no matter how much I like the last one!

I fear that such an ideal political world will not exist for a while yet, if at all. But if we can't find it on the road to our parliament, then it might be harder still to find it in the parliament itself. While PR may make majorities less likely and co-operation more necessary, it may not in itself heal the wounds that endless conflict has created – but then again it *might* heal them because, paradoxically, the fight is at its most bitter where the similarities are most obvious. Whilst 'new' Labour is very much out of tune with what Scotland wants – providing in Andrew Marr's recent perceptive analysis a relaunch of 19th-century Liberalism, original and enduring Labour values in Scotland are to be found as strongly in the SNP as anywhere else. Values that express community worth (there *is* such a thing as 'society'), shared responsibility, egalitarianism, and a belief in 'progress' that does not exclude or disbar or impoverish – all those things still live on in some parts of the Labour Party in Scotland, and live on in the SNP.

The SNP's contribution in the 80s and 90s has been to relate those values to the modern world and particularly to Europe, and to formulate a way in which such values could be effectively expressed in and by Scotland. Those in Labour who share these values have had to make endless compromises and to swallow a diktat that declares them old fashioned, out of touch and impossible to achieve. The fact that they have been supported by the vast majority of Scots for a generation seems irrelevant to Downing Street today, just as it was then.

Muir saw the challenge facing Scotland in 1934 as being a choice between the continuation of capitalism and a socialism that would value people before profit. He rejected nationalism because it did not insist on that dichotomy: 'A hundred years of Socialism would do more to restore Scotland to health and weld it into a real nation than a thousand years – if that were conceivable – of Nationalist government such as that to which the National Party of Scotland looks forward; for even if the country were governed by Scotsmen, the economic conflicts within it could still generate the same intestine hatreds as they do now, and would still deserve to do so.'

But Muir's vision needs both elements – for he goes on to write: 'Looking, then, at Scotland as impartially as I could, in the little room of the hotel on that last evening of my run, I seemed to see that it was ripe for two things: to become a nation and to become a Socialist community; but I could not see it becoming the one without becoming the other.'

Muir's conclusions have a contemporary relevance, but also a distancing effect. His insistence that what Scotland needed was to be changed '...by Socialists and Douglasites. And it is necessary that it should be changed by them. Scotland needs a hundred years of Douglasism to sweat out of it the individualism which destroyed it as a nation and has brought it where it is' seems bizarre today when we have forgotten what Douglasism was.

But one could express what Muir concluded in today's terms without losing much of the sense of it – one could update it to take account of the political and social changes and argue that Scotland needs not just its independence, but also the strong values of its past and the deep and abiding belief in a more equal, more just, more compassionate society which has been the hallmark of Scottish politics this century.

And if that is so, then does not the task of building that society become one that should engage not just one political party, but those in all political parties who share that aim? Does it not almost dictate the need for the realignment of Scottish politics which has seemed for so long to be only just out of reach? Realignments, of course, do not take place in the middle of battlefields. This present electoral war will have to be fought and won on the present ground, and no doubt with the political weapons which have been forged and tempered in the Westminster school. But as we undertake that task we should not lose sight of the many things that unite some of the combatants, and the fact that working together in our new parliament – and only working together in our new parliament – can make those things real.

I have always believed that working together in that way will make independence more likely, rather than less likely. For the basic question then becomes one of achieving the shared aims, and that is simply not possible if Scotland remains within the United Kingdom, and at arms length from Europe and the world.

In all of the joint campaigns in which I have participated I have never once found that my conviction for independence was undermined or weakened. On the contrary, the need for independence has become self-evident to those who did not share it, and who have invested too much in the old ways to be able to change quickly. They have left such campaigns privately acknowledging that independence will come and must come – but they have always found ways of saying that something (devolution, social justice, more jobs, better housing) needs to come first. One by one those arguments are disappearing – independence will come, because – as Muir himself saw – it needs to come.

And Muir was right to see that it should not, and would not, come alone. It will come with – during, before and after – the social and economic changes that are also needed. Muir's Scotland was not yet ready for those changes. 'The National Party', he writes, 'has nothing behind it but a desire and nothing before it but an ideal; and it is numerically so weak as to be negligible.' He goes on: 'These are facts that no amount of publicity and no degree of romanticising of realities can alter.'

Sixty-four years later these observations are no longer

true. Behind us lies a record of solid electoral achievement and experience of running local councils and of involvement in the political process. Before us lies a concrete opportunity to build a new parliament, buttressed by a political programme that is detailed, pragmatic and born of experience. Romanticisation is something that we have given up these many years – I have even been criticised by journalists for being for too prosaic in my approach – and our constant economic expositions make even economic correspondents quail. And although we are still good at publicity, the attention we get is now commensurate with the seriousness of our challenge.

Is his further challenge more difficult to dispute? For he says that 'I have tried to approach the Scottish Nationalist movement as sympathetically as possible; I saw in my journey through Scotland the justification for it; I still see that its object is admirable. But there are numberless movements that are justified in themselves and whose objects are admirable, and only one or two in any age which can prevail, because they come out of the deeper life that creates history. I think that in a Douglasite or Socialist Britain Scotland would be given liberty to govern itself; but I cannot think of its achieving nationality in any other way; and a parliament in Edinburgh made up of the Scottish members at present sitting in Westminster is not an ideal which can inspire a deep passion.'

The idea of a mini-Westminster, full of the present Labour back benches still fails to inspire passion – that is not what Scotland wants from its new democratic beating heart. But does the present 'national' movement come out – at last – from the deeper life of Scotland that creates history? Can it prevail as one of the forces of the age that will shape our country? Only if it recognises that it is not an end in itself – or rather that it is both an end and a means, and that the means is as important as the end.

The time is right now for progress towards the national, the economic and the social system we wish to create –

towards all of them, together. That social system is of itself very different from what Muir wanted, but it is one that accords with the reality of the world, the opportunities of globalisation and the resources of our country. It also accords with what has happened since Muir made his journey – the success of capitalism in spreading its benefits more widely. Scotland is a better place than the one Muir drove through. But it is not as good as it could be, and it cannot be further improved without the type of change that he wanted, albeit expressed and executed in modern terms.

Some of the changes took place in Muir's lifetime. George Bruce, the poet, was a friend of Muir's and when I spoke to him in his spruce Edinburgh house he drew attention to Muir's 'abstract' qualities and to the opinion of Muir's extrovert wife that he wrote nothing memorable until he was 55, and that all his poems thereafter – with one exception – were 'abstracts': indeed at times almost abstracted out of meaning or existence.

Scottish Journey is not an abstract book. Written when he was 48 it deals with hard realities and with concrete solutions to human problems. Perhaps his realisation that some of these solutions were impractical or impossible lay behind his failure to mention *Scottish Journey* in his *An Autobiography*. George Bruce thinks he virtually disowned it, having moved on from that phase of his life into one of abstract ideas, symbols and allegory. He may also have regretted some of the more critical passages, particularly his sharp denunciation of Glasgow and Lanarkshire. These were personal reactions, not part of a thesis.

And we must not forget TS Eliot's description of Muir as 'the boy from a simple, primitive, offshore community who...was plunged into the sordid horror of industrialism... who struggled to understand the modern world of the metropolis'. *Scottish Journey* has strong elements of a psychological coming-to-terms with the modern world, and that experience – that catharsis – colours much of the observation. Bruce describes Muir as 'a displaced person' and it was only in his latter years as Warden of Newbattle Abbey College that he found the way in which he could most perfectly relate to the world: a way in which he acted as the enabler for others to make progress.

Muir in conversation was apparently quiet and reserved. But, according to George Bruce, he would suddenly add to any discussion some 'simple and shrewd points...points that showed how aware he was of the complexities of life'. *Scottish Journey* is, without doubt, his longest statement on the nation from which he sprung. Yet at times it possesses that simple shrewdness others observed in him in other circumstances.

Writing, like a company's annual audit, is a snapshot. It is the truth of the moment as one sees it and the moment changes. The remark that fits in a book may not fit in a political pamphlet and will certainly not fit in a poem, but *Scottish Journey* is not a book to be disowned. It is a strong and radical approach to a moment of Scotland's past and although this book is about the present and future, that too will be behind us ere long, and its errors of judgement and analysis (even unconscious ones) will be available for scrutiny and rejection. And no doubt its perspective, and mine, will be called to account.

But, for the moment, what have I really learnt from my Scottish journey?

Firstly, that Scotland is diverse and each of the parts that I visited has strengths and weaknesses. It is a small country in geographical terms, but, as Muir said, in the course of any journey one will come into contact with 'various Scotlands, passing from one into another without rhyme or reason.' Some of these Scotlands are doing better than others, but all of them have – in places and not consistently – needs and hopes which they are looking to the parliament to fulfil.

Secondly, that despite the differences, Scotland is also a unity. What seem to be needs peculiar to one place have echoes or similarities wherever one goes. Drugs and crime in Glasgow are not replicated exactly in Golspie or Galashiels – but the frustration of youth unemployment, the decline of society and its cohesion and the emptiness of lives lived in poverty are common factors in many of our towns and cities. In one place it may be murder and mayhem – in another the smashing of windows. Both are symptoms of the same sickness and need a cure rather than just condemnation.

And as with social exclusion, so with homelessness, crumbling schools, failing health and inadequate transport systems. Some problems may be worse in the Highlands, but they are not just Highland problems: they are problems that as a nation we must solve.

Thirdly, I have learnt that we do have opportunities – keen and energetic people, individuals working tirelessly for community good. And overall a population that wants to see not only themselves, but also their neighbours do well. We may have missed the boat in 1979, but it has come back to harbour in 1997. We seem, or most of us seem, determined not to fail ourselves once more.

There are things too that I did not find in my travels. This is not Poland or Croatia or South Africa or any other country keen to rid itself of its oppressor and rise up again. We were not, and have not been, colonised and occupied, at least in any conventionally understood way.

Tom Nairn memorably described the Scots as a 'self-colonised' people – we have accepted the mores and the political domination of our neighbours because that seemed the best way forward. Now it is beginning to seem that there might be a better way. We will try that out, taking our steps cautiously and travelling hopefully before we arrive anywhere else. We are not given to great outbursts of flag waving, or to demonstrating in the city squares. Even our football supporters prefer camaraderie and an inclusive, entertaining, partying sort of pride to the aggressive nationalism that seems to be rising south of the border.

We do not regard ourselves as better than anyone else. 'Wha's like us' is an old music hall boast. It has few adherents in the modern Scotland. What we want is to be the same as anyone else – to be equal with others and make our modest way in the world on our own virtues rather than on the coat tails of others with different qualities.

In other words Scotland *has* grown up. Muir saw its growing pains – its poverty and depression and its confusion about where it should go. Somehow we came through it, and now stand more comfortably, more at ease with ourselves.

Another traveller, setting out today on the same journey, might find something different. But for me this politically inconsistent, understated, ambitious, inwardly strong, complex personality of our nation is the biggest revelation. It is far more mature than many of our politicians appear to believe. It will no longer be frightened out of its future, or kept in line by carrots or sticks. It is, rather patiently, prepared to wait for what is coming, and to try out what it creates from its new chances.

As I was finishing this book, my publisher's Autumn 1998 catalogue arrived in the mail. There was the blurb I had helped prepare so many months ago, and there was a cover design that I thought had not yet been finalised. But as I looked longer at Gus Wylie's photograph it dawned on me that the 'KEEP OUT' sign is a good illustration for the story I have told. (Gus Wylie took that photograph in Skye in 1975, forty years after *Scottish Journey* had been published.) For too long Scotland has kept the world at bay. Too few have understood what has been happening here, and how we have been changing. Our image overseas is festooned with tartan or daubed in face paint and our self-image has been corrupted by the reflection of those projected images.

Edwin Muir told a different tale when he looked into our nation in 1934. I have tried to do the same. The old 'KEEP OUT' sign has rotted away. We should brush it aside and let the world see who we are now.

And who we might be once the waiting is over.